I would like to dedicate this work to all those who, in one way or another inspired me to write it : my parents (I never got round to telling them how loving they were), my brothers and sisters and their families, and all those I have encountered on my way through life.

ISBN: 978-1-84944-024-0

British Library Cataloguing in Publication Data.
A catalogue record for this book is available from the British Library.

Published by UKUnpublished

www.ukunpublished.co.uk
info@ukunpublished.co.uk

THE GOSPEL MAKES SENSE

By

Rev. Bernard O'Connor OSA

The Gospel Makes Sense

Contents

PREFACE

This book was begun during a period of enforced leisure but is the result of a long period of musings often formulated in homilies at Mass and elsewhere. It also realises dreamy resolutions one day to put pen to paper – or to be thoroughly modern, to touch the keys of the computer.

It is aimed at those who are vaguely interested in religion in the broadest sense of the word, but who have been alienated by a bad experience or inaccurate teaching. Yet I found myself giving advice to priests at the end of one chapter, so there might be something there for them, too.

I am now in my 80s (an age when one starts boasting about it!), have been an Augustinian for over 60 years and a priest for over 50 years. In that time I have grown in appreciation of the Gospel of Jesus Christ. The spirit of his teaching, his interaction with people, everything about his personality is so inspiring, so beautiful, so positive.

The content of this book is based on a lifetime of endeavouring to communicate that spirit in a variety of pastoral experiences: in a secondary school, a stage of life when youngsters ask the most difficult and awkward questions, then in various parishes, where I encountered not only the parishioners, but people of all faiths and none.

It has often struck me what strange and sad ideas many people have of what we Christians believe. I am sometimes astonished at the inaccuracies one encounters in newspaper columns, when the writer is referring to Catholic beliefs and practices. Even practising Christians can have some malformed notions. If one may say so, priests have been known to continue to work on an amalgam of ideas long since gone stale and tired. The following chapters endeavour to correct a few basic misapprehensions.

Some good Catholic people have difficulties with aspects of the Church's teaching. They find themselves sometimes on the horns of a dilemma. No matter which way they move it appears they will be wrong! I cannot claim to be able to resolve intractable problems, but perhaps something here might help bring them peace of mind. The point of reference, the criterion is always the Gospel.

A priest meets people intimately at crucial periods of their lives, especially weddings, baptisms and funerals. Many people do not fit neatly into the patterns and categories that the Church would regard as ideal. Nevertheless one is confronted with goodwill, with an honest desire to do what is right and, where there is a newborn child, to ensure the child grows up well – not making the same mistakes its parents made! Being confronted with such earnestness concentrates the mind and, for me, helped me to clarify lots of things for myself, which I would like to share.

I can only write from what I know, that is, as a Roman Catholic. That is not to dismiss the other great churches and religions. Each one has something special to teach us. Each one, in its own different way is seeking truth and goodness, a journey and a desire that we all share. I have learnt too from people of no specific religious persuasion who raised questions about issues of religious belief and set me thinking about some, perhaps simplistic assumptions I had been making. We all benefit by listening to each other with open heart and mind. The following chapters are my effort to contribute to the conversation.

The book deals with a few fundamental topics, but in no way are the subjects exhausted. It is hoped that these brief essays might open doors for those for whom they have been slammed shut and may stimulate them to investigate further.

I have tried to be honest and to face the difficult questions, but the reader will decide. In composing the text, I sat down at the computer and typed, consulting only a few rough notes I had made, with the essential points and occasionally checking references. I referred to articles I wrote and to homilies I have preached – with my increasingly porous memory I have taken to writing them out in full.

I cannot give a complete bibliography. I did not keep a card-index system over the years, filing references and quotes that impressed me. I had not planned to sit down one day and write a book. It might just happen that somebody reads and recognises here something he/she had written once upon a time, without it being acknowledged. I hope such a one will be compensated by knowing that the thought and inspiration once committed to print meant something to somebody, who managed to integrate it into his concept of life, faith, religion.

What follows comes off the top of my head, and, I hope, from my heart. I pray that it may appeal to the head and reach the heart of everyone who reads it.

Bernard O'Connor OSA.

1. RELIGION

'They're all hypocrites', he said after a pint too many when the subject under discussion was religion, 'every one of them.' Others would repeat a similar opinion when cold sober.

'Religion' must be the most misunderstood word and concept that there is. Even well educated people, to judge by what is sometimes written in newspaper columns, even people who are genuinely religious, can have the most weird ideas of what it means.

'An Oppressive Influence; the Cause of Violence'

It is seen by some as an oppressive influence, often used by priests, parents and teachers to exert control over others and get their submission, always associated with 'don't', 'thou shalt not'. These associations and their childhood experiences can alienate people to an extent that lasts a lifetime. Religion, however, properly understood is a positive and constructive influence in the world.

Religion also has been associated with creating hostile factions, whose antipathies sometimes explode into violence. Northern Ireland: Protestant versus Catholic; the Middle East: Jew versus Muslim, are two sad examples of modern times. Most threatening of all is the alienation of so many Muslims from what they perceive to be the Christian west, bringing with it the constant fear of terrorism, the use of violence in waging 'war' against terrorists, indeed the blanket classification of a whole section of the population as potential terrorists.

Nowhere in the Gospel, however, will one find any justification for taking up arms or inflicting violence in the name of Jesus Christ. Quite the contrary. As Pope John Paul II said in Drogheda in 1979 at the height of the 'troubles' in Northern Ireland, 'Nowhere in the Gospel will you read "you shall murder your brother", or "you shall hate your neighbour".'

Even a superficial reflection will show that violence explodes not because of shades of religious belief but because of issues such as demands for human rights or competing for power, land, oil, minerals and possibly and fearfully, water. It sometimes lends respectability to a cause and rallies support for it, to justify it in the name of religion, when the real motives are clearly otherwise. All that is needed is to demonise the other side and hence to show that we are fighting for the good. Therefore God is on our side!

Religion: the Reality

Religion came about as a result of human endeavour from the beginning of time to make sense of the world. It was a gradual evolution. The wisdom of each age was passed on from generation to generation. Crude notions of the reality of the world were gradually refined. Good and evil were identified by what resonates with human instincts and what repels. 'Good' became identified with what promotes the well-being of the individual and of the community, while 'Evil' is the opposite. Gradually a rational basis for distinguishing between good and evil was developed, from which codes of morality emerged. It became clear that, in order to live together in harmony, everybody had to recognise that others too have rights which must be respected.

One of the outstanding contributions of the Jewish faith to human values is its insistence on justice for all, with special regard for the weakest and most vulnerable among us. This is emphasised in the elaboration of the ten commandments in the Old Testament(1), and is central to the teachings and practice of Jesus in the New Testament. Concern for the weak is not something that human beings naturally regard as a priority in their lives. Religion, however insists that it is a priority.

Religion in its broadest sense is not confined to any one group or to church membership. There are occasions and happenings which are awesome and which, even in the most secular language can be described as 'sacred'. Examples are when a father holds his first new-born baby for the first time; or when a woman and man pledge themselves to each other in marriage for the rest of their lives, come what may; or when nurses care with great gentleness and patience for the infirm of body or mind. These are some of many such examples that can truly be described as 'sacred', whether the people concerned describe themselves as religious or not. They are moments when the human being is seen at its best, male and female, when one reaches beyond self-interest and engages in what can only be called 'love'.

Making Sense of the World: Basic Questions

The Old Testament of the Bible describes the efforts of our ancestors to make sense of the world in which they lived. Genesis is the first book of the Bible and its first eleven chapters are an account of human effort to answer basic questions, questions that still exercise our minds even in our sophisticated age.

How did the world come about?
How to explain the human tendency to evil?
Why do people speak different languages?
How to explain failure and suffering?

Genesis answers them by telling stories: creation by God, Adam and Eve our first parents, the tower of Babel, the flood and Noah's ark.

These events are described in the early chapters of the Bible   Are they historical or are they stories told to illustrate a fundamental issue? Even today the argument continues, with a small but increasingly vocal group insisting on the historical nature of the early chapters of Genesis.

The Bible does not offer answers to questions such as 'Why?' 'How' and 'why' express curiosity, a healthy and intelligent curiosity that has led to the growth of human understanding of the workings of the world, but curiosity nonetheless. It is a constructive curiosity that follows avenues of discovery in order to enable humankind use the resources of the planet that the Creator has endowed so abundantly. The Bible tells us what we need to know in order to lead a good life, and leaves it to human imagination and ingenuity to answer questions of 'how' and 'why'.

Creation and Evolution

Those who insist on the literal interpretation of the first chapters of Genesis are known as 'creationists' in contrast to 'evolutionists'. The word 'creationist' may give the impression that anyone who believes that the world was created by God (of Whom more later) denies the possibility of evolution. In fact there is no contradiction between believing that God created the world in its primitive form, and that the world gradually evolved to what we have today. Charles Darwin concludes the second edition of his classic 'The Origin of Species' with the following sentence: *'There is grandeur in this view of life with its several powers* (i.e. evolution) *having been originally breathed by the Creator into a few forms or one ..... from so simple a beginning endless forms most beautiful and wonderful have been, and are being evolved.'* The words *'by the Creator'* were inserted in the second edition, possibly in response to the outcry that greeted the first edition. For Darwin, if not for some of his successors, it seems creation by God and gradual evolution are perfectly compatible.

Pope John Paul II said in an address to the Pontifical Academy of Sciences on 22 October 1996: *'In his encyclical* "Humani Generis" *(1950), my predecessor Pius XII has already affirmed that there is no conflict between evolution and the doctrine of the faith regarding man and his vocation, provided that we do not lose sight of certain fixed points....Today, more than a half-century after the appearance of that encyclical, some new findings lead us toward the recognition of evolution as more than an hypothesis.'*(2)

From the beginning the beauty and wonder of the world has been recognised. The first chapter of Genesis is sheer poetry, describing the various stages of creation and how at each stage, like a refrain, 'God saw that it was good'. Everything in the world is good, and can be developed by humans for the general well-being, but sadly can also be manipulated and used for evil purposes.

Older people will remember the first time a photograph of our planet was sent back to us from space – how we gasped in wonder at this beautiful, blue and white sphere alone in space, so strategically positioned that it gets enough sun but not too much, moving around the sun in such a way as to vary the seasons. An endless cycle of evaporation, clouds, rain, provides an abundance of water – life-giving water, without which there is only desert.

Our planet not only produces everything that we need in abundance, but it is also so beautiful: the trees, the rivers, the fields, the mountains, the sky, the stars and the rotation of seasons, each one with its character and purpose. The earth nourishes us with food and drink, it fills our lungs with air, it is warmed by the sun and cooled by the breeze, rain fills our rivers , our lakes, our wells ....

The Bible

For Christians, the source of their understanding of religion is the Bible. The Old Testament from the twelfth chapter of Genesis onwards, is the story of a particular group of people, the descendants of Abraham. They were chosen by God to be His people for a special purpose.

Abraham and Moses are described as having direct encounters with God. Such direct encounters with God are outside the experience of all but a privileged few and are difficult to imagine. They can be judged only by what they contribute to the well-being of humanity.

The Bible describes how God 'called' Abraham, to gather his family and what he needed for a long journey, and to set out for a land where he would settle. God promised that he would become the father of a great nation, that his descendants would be as numerous as the stars, even though Abraham and his wife, Sarah were childless and elderly. Abraham never seems to have doubted the promises made to him and accepted obediently whatever God seemed to ask of him. Eventually, we are told they did have a child, Isaac. It is no wonder that Abraham is described as 'our father in faith'.

The Bible later describes the encounters of God with Moses, where Moses is instructed what to do. His first task was to lead his people out of Egypt to the promised land, a land 'filled with milk and honey'. The 'Exodus' became and remains one of the great celebrated events in the history of the Jewish people. Later Moses would receive the ten commandments from God on Mount Sinai.

The ten commandments are a summary of the wisdom gleaned through the generations and handed down through the ages. The fourth to the tenth commandments express the basic human rights of others, which must be respected if people are to live together in harmony – respect for the life, the person, the property, the good name of others, not only in our actions but also in our hearts.

God's chosen people, eventually known as 'the Israelites' had a chequered history. The Old Testament describes wars, battles and a lot of violence, perpetrated by the Israelites, who believed God was on their side. This puzzles and repels many. 'What about the other people?' they understandably ask. The overall story, however, is an account of the struggle between Good and Evil. But the writers of the time did not use abstractions like Good and Evil, rather there are good people (i.e. us) and bad people (them). They reasoned that God must be on the side of the good people, but when they get a bloody nose in battle, they cannot understand it. In that case, their holy men attribute their failure, as they did all suffering, to their sinfulness and infidelity.

It is a very crude understanding of reality, which became refined as time went on, as the later books of the Old Testament make clear. An example of that refinement occurs early on, when Abraham is told to offer his only son, Isaac in sacrifice. Obedient as always, he proceeded to do so, and it was only when he was about to light the byre to which his son was tied, that his hand was stayed.(3) The story illustrates that human sacrifice, apparently practised at the time, was not acceptable to God.

The Bible describes the evolution of religion, from bewildered beginnings, human wisdom enlightened by God's promptings gradually leading to the Gospels, which are the inspiration for Christians, challenging them to a way of living that is best described as 'Love your neighbour as yourself.' Your neighbour is every person, not just one of the chosen few. It is a way that is personified in Jesus (of whom more later), who said that he had come, not to set aside the law, but to perfect it.

There is a thread that runs through the Bible, from the beginning, through the Old Testament (the Hebrew Bible as it is also known) to the New Testament that is hard to describe. 'Consistency' is probably the best word. Scripture scholars point out how events and prophecies of the Old find their parallels in the New. They are not scientific proofs but somehow it all seems to hang together.

Other aspects of the Bible are indicated in a later chapter.

....

Religion is wisdom, the wisdom that enables us distinguish right from wrong, good from evil and that urges us to choose what is right and what is good, to reject what is wrong and what is evil. It is practised to a much greater extent than is usually acknowledged. Popes often recognise this fact when they address themselves to 'all people of good will'. Religion, however implicit suggests transcending self and exclusive self-interest and recognising a higher principle that guides one's life.

Religion, of course in its strictest sense, centres on the divine and not only recognises but worships God. The first three of the ten commandments are centred on God. God. Now there is another word, concept, reality, person that is gravely misunderstood.

1. Deuteronomy 10:18,19 'justice for the fatherless, the widow .. love for the stranger.'
2. 'The Genesis Enigma' by Andrew Parker (Doubleday 2009) shows how the order of creation described in Genesis 1 is precisely how the world would have evolved. He suggests this extraordinary foresight is evidence of divine inspiration.
3. Genesis c.22.

2. GOD

The notion of God is a stumbling block for many. There are all
sorts of images: an old man with a beard up there somewhere;
less attractively, an ogre who sees everything, records everything
and will punish every little transgression, or one who allows all
sorts of pain and suffering and does nothing to alleviate it.
Sometimes, when reading descriptions of God even by well-
educated people and their notions of what we believe God to be,
one is not surprised that they call themselves atheists.

Images of God

It is virtually impossible to describe God. Words are inadequate.
Indeed as soon as we use words, we are circumscribing God
within our imagination, our concepts, our experiences. Still, we
can but talk and write about God, seeking to know about Him and
to know Him a little better.

We say 'Him' and already there is a distortion, because God is not
masculine rather than feminine. Using 'Him' rather than 'Her' is a
convention inherited from a male dominated world. It illustrates
the poverty of our language, which has not a relevant pronoun
independent of gender. In order to avoid tedious repetition of
'him/her', we shall stick with the convention.

Different people conceive of God in their different ways, based on
images they received as they grew up or through their own
reflections and prayer. These images might be tested against the
Bible, and in particular against the Gospel. Just as with words,
when we form a concept of God in our imagination, we are
limiting Him to what our imagination can contain. But that
should not deter us. It is the best we can do. It would be an

arrogant person who would insist that his or her image of God is the only correct one. It is no disgrace to be inarticulate when attempting to speak of God. 'There must be something else' is as good a description as 'signs of transcendence'.

Many of our images of God come from the Old Testament. The Old Testament is an account of the gradual growth of human awareness of God and of God's nature. People realised that there were forces outside their control, for example the weather, on which they depended so much for their crops and, hence their existence.

God, a Person

This force, for the Israelites, was seen from the beginning as a person. Just as good and evil were personalised as good people and bad people, so too this 'force' was a person. In the beginning, the person was regarded as awesome and had to be placated by offerings and sacrifices –even by human sacrifices. Gradually, however, they became aware whether through revelations or through the inspirations of holy men, that God did not need human beings or even animals sacrificed to Him – He could provide for His own needs, thank you very much. What He did ask for was a humble and contrite heart. Later writers and preachers spoke of the Lord as *'kind and full of compassion, slow to anger and rich in mercy.*(1)

Because He was a person, the Israelites spoke to Him. At times, they praised Him, in awe at the rich and beautiful world He had given them; at times they pondered good and evil, mystified especially when bad people seemed to prosper and good people (like themselves) seemed to suffer; at times they complained bitterly when God seemed to take no notice of their prayers and their needs, when He seemed to be asleep! Always, God was real for them, even when they ignored Him, complained about Him or wandered away from Him. Always, too they had supreme trust in Him, that whatever the present difficulties, He would see to it that all would be right in the end. All of these various attitudes are expressed in the Book of Psalms, the collection of their traditional prayers and hymns.

The Law of God

Likewise, the law of God came to be recognised, not as an imposition from outside but as wisdom. When Moses gave the ten commandments to the people, along with threats of the consequences of disobeying he added *'Keep them, put them into practice, and other peoples will admire your wisdom and prudence.'* (Deuteronomy, 4:6) *'Let these words be written on your hearts' (Deuteronomy 6:7),* he wrote as he proclaimed the first commandment of love of God. Later the prophet Jeremiah writes: *'The Lord declares:…Within them, I shall plant my Law, writing it on their hearts …. they will all know me, from the least to the greatest, since I shall forgive their guilt and never more call their sin to mind.'* (31:34) The Law shall be 'written on their hearts' because they shall realise that it resonates with all their better instincts. These are not rules, not penal laws imposed from outside, but words of wisdom that express an orientation of one's whole outlook on life.

In modern times, the Law of God has been described as 'the manufacturer's instructions' for human existence. Human beings are, of course free to ignore them, but if they do, they must not be surprised at the unpleasant consequences. It is as if one chooses to put water in the petrol tank of a car, on the grounds that 'It is <u>my</u> car. I can do what I like with it.' Of course you can, but don't blame the manufacturer for the subsequent disaster!

However much the Law was presented as wisdom, the fear of God persisted, fear of being punished for doing wrong, fear that suffering was a consequence of having done wrong in the past. Even today, suffering is sometimes seen as a punishment. People who live a blameless life ask 'What did we do to deserve this?' We shall see later how Jesus dealt with this question.(2)

It must be admitted too that through the years, preachers whose eloquence was greater than their familiarity with the Gospels, used fearful images of God, threatening hell and damnation to the sinner, in order to stir their congregation to repentance. Priests, teachers, parents have used the threat of the all-seeing God to inspire fear and keep congregations and children in line. Even a superficial reading of the Gospels shows God in a different light.

Love of God

The first commandment, known as the 'Shema' became as basic to the Israelites' expression of faith as the 'Our Father' is to Christians. *'Listen, Israel: The Lord our God is the one, the only Lord. You shall love the Lord your God with all your heart, with all your soul, with all your strength. Let these words I urge on you today be written on your hearts. You shall tell them to your children ...... you shall fasten them on your hand as a sign and on your forehead as a headband; you shall write them on the doorposts of your house and on your gates.'* (Deuteronomy 6:4-9). No doubt the modern equivalent of the headband would be the T-shirt.

But how can one be expected to 'love' God when one cannot see Him, or even imagine Him? It is perhaps significant that in the English language the words 'God' and 'Good' are so closely related. To 'love' is to see the object of one's love as desirable, valued, sought after. Hence to love God is to see as desirable, valued and sought after, whatever is godly, that is, whatever is good and true and beautiful. God is described as the One who is the perfection of all Goodness.

Every person who performs a good and generous act reflects the image of God, even though other aspects of that person's life may be less than edifying. The Samaritan woman that Jesus met at Jacob's Well is an example. (3) So, the reflection of God can be found all about us, sometimes in the most unexpected people. Those who endeavour in their lives to be guided by the desire for what is good and true and beautiful are, perhaps unwittingly, expressing love of God.

St John, in his first letter says: *His commandment is this, that we believe in the name of his Son Jesus Christ and that we should love each other as he commanded us. Whoever keeps his commandments remains in God and God in him.* (3:23) Even those who cannot yet 'believe in the name of his Son', if they endeavour to live a good life, are well on the way.

When the New Testament speaks of a 'commandment' to love God, to love our neighbour, it uses the word in a metaphoric, even ironic sense. 'Which is the greatest commandment?' Jesus is asked. The only 'commandment' that I give you is love God, love one another. One cannot be 'commanded' to love. Love cannot be imposed by an outside authority, no matter how great, but can only be a free and inner response from the heart, from the depths of one's conviction and commitment.

The Prophet Elijah seeking an encounter with God found Him not in the mighty wind, nor in the earthquake, nor in the fire but rather in the *'still, small voice'*.(4) The still, small voice is a reality for every human being, the voice of conscience, whispering gently within us. It is described in modern terms:

'In the depths of his conscience, man detects a law which he does not impose upon himself, but which holds him to obedience. Always summoning him to love good and avoid evil, the voice of conscience can when necessary speak to the heart more specifically: do this, shun that. For man has in his heart a law written by God. To obey it is the very dignity of man; according to it he will be judged.

Conscience is the most secret core and sanctuary of a man. There he is alone with God, whose voice echoes in his depths. In a wonderful manner conscience reveals that law which is fulfilled by love of God and love of neighbour.' (5)

Our Father

Jesus came, as he said, not to do away with the Law as handed down through the generations, but to perfect it. He gave us the ultimate image of God: Our Father. This title is not to emphasise the masculine, but rather expresses the Good Parent, embracing all the best qualities of the good mother and the good father. This means loving each one of the children as they are, individually and separately. Some of the children may behave badly and reject home and family, but the good parent is always there for them, to clasp them to their hearts when they return. (It might be encouraging for parents to reflect that when Jesus was looking for an image of God, he could think of none better than the good parent.)

Jesus addressed God as 'Abba', the child's way of speaking to his/her father. Our equivalent would be 'Dad'. How would we feel about addressing God as Dad? Embarrassed, no doubt. Perhaps that is a sign that we have not yet quite reached the state described by St Paul in both his letter to the Galatians (chapter 4) and his letter to the Romans (chapter 8), where he suggests that to be able from our hearts to address God as 'Abba' shows that we have understood and absorbed everything the Gospel teaches.

It is not the word that matters but rather the deep-seated attitudes and convictions based on a life of faith that gives us an insight into the real nature of God and enables us to be free and easy in His presence.

'Proofs' of God's Existence

The Old Testament insists there is but one God. The people of Israel never seem to have questioned the fact, though they often incurred the wrath of their prophets by behaving as if there were no God. Other civilisations of the time formed idols before which they paid tribute as their recognition that there is 'someone' entitled to their respect and worship.

Philosophers have pondered the existence of God, often in response to controversies. Nowadays we would talk of 'proof', used in a scientific sense of studying the material, visible, quantifiable evidence and drawing an undeniable conclusion. It is not that simple.

St Anselm describes 'that than which no greater can be imagined' and St Thomas Aquinas produced what are often referred to as the 'five proofs'. That was not St Thomas's description. He referred to the 'Five Ways'. What the philosophers establish is that belief in God is at least reasonable, something that an intelligent, thinking person can accept.

A modern consideration is based on the extraordinary order of the universe, whereby the location of a planet or star can be accurately calculated for any moment of its history, past, present or future. The argument goes that to suggest this came about by chance would be the equivalent of the contents of a scrap yard being thrown together haphazardly and a Jumbo Jet emerging. (6)

The same holds for human reason as does for words and images. If there were a simple, unanswerable proof for God's existence, it would suggest that God can be contained within the limits of human reason, which would be a contradiction in terms. It would also mean that there would be no atheists!

Everybody has a 'god', something which they regard as the most important thing in their lives, for which they are often prepared to sacrifice everything else. It may be money, career, prestige, power, self-indulgence, for which they have an insatiable appetite. These are their idols. But it is the pursuit of goodness, truth, honesty that leads to the one, true God.

One of the great stories of the search for the fullness of Truth is the *Confessions* of St Augustine, still, after 1600 years, on the shelves of serious bookshops.

'What is my God?' he asks. *'I put my question to the earth ... the sea and the chasms of the deep and the living things that creep in them .. the wind ... , the sky, the sun, the moon and the stars and they told me "We are not your God.' ... and I said "Since you are not my God, tell me about him .." Clear and loud they answered "God is he who made us." I asked these questions simply by gazing at these things, and their beauty was all the answer they gave.'* (7)

A Leap of Faith.

However much one may rationalise about the reality of God, about relating to God as Father, about recognising Jesus as Son of God who took on our human nature, about being aware of God's abiding presence among us in his Spirit, all of this requires at some stage a leap of faith. However convinced the intellect may be, there comes a time for an act of the will, an affective act, a time to close one's eyes and jump, confident that one will land in the arms of a loving Father.

St. Augustine spent from his adolescence to his thirty-third year, anxiously looking for the truth. Even when he found what he recognised as the truth, he baulked at its implications for his way of life. It was some time before he could bring himself to take the irreversible step of asking for baptism. That brought him to the end of a long journey, and the beginning of a new and exciting stage of his life, which has influenced philosophy and theology in the western world ever since.

'I found my God, who is Truth itself,' he writes, *'when I found truth.*(8) *'You were within me, and I was in the world outside myself. I searched for you outside myself and, disfigured as I was, I fell upon the lovely things of your creation. You were with me, but I was not with you.'* (9) It could, with good reason be argued that those who earnestly search for God have already found Him.

The modern mind is uncomfortable with the notion of 'mystery', that which is not simply something over the horizon which our understanding will reach eventually, but rather that which is greater than and beyond the capacity of our comprehension. Sometimes it seems that the only adequate response to the mystery of God is to go on our knees in a cloud of unknowing and, in humble awareness, to whisper into the darkness 'Our Father'.

1. Psalms 103:6, 144:8
2. See Chapter 10 'Difficult Questions: Suffering'
3. See John chapter 4.
4. 1 Kings 19:12
5. Vatican Council II: 'The Church Today, n.16. (Women readers please understand this document was written before awareness of the need for inclusive language.)
6. 'The Genesis Enigma' however, finds this argument faulty cf. pages 76,77.
7. St Augustine 'Confessions' Book X:6 (Penguin Classics).
8. 'Confessions' X:24.
9. 'Confessions' X:27.

3. JESUS

*'And what is it,' she asked me, 'that keeps you going?' She was a
professional woman, dedicated to the people she served, much loved by
them for her gentle ministry, often going beyond the call of duty. She
was a regular at church. Recently, she had been through a hard time
with family bereavements. Then religion seemed to die for her, not out of
anger or bitterness; it just dried up. I talked to her, though knowing that
words would not be sufficient. Then she asked me 'And what is it that
keeps you going?' My response was immediate: 'Jesus, the man as we
find him in the Gospels.'*

*I can remember the time when I realised that our Christian faith is not a
code of rules which we are bound to obey, nor is it a creed of dogmas to
which we are bound to give intellectual assent. Rather it is a person,
Jesus Christ who, even through the pages of Gospels that are 2000 years
and more old, radiates warmth, gentleness, strength, authority, goodness.
That was a time when a light suddenly shone for me that lit up all sorts
of dark corners.*

Let us try to put aside all our preconceptions about Jesus, look at
the man that emerges from the Gospels of Matthew, Mark and
Luke, and see where that takes us. They described the life of
Jesus, what he did, what he said, how he interacted with people
and expected that we would conclude that he was indeed the
Messiah, the holy one of God.

An Ordinary Home Background

One remarkable detail is that when Jesus preached in his home
town, the local people were astonished. 'Where did he get this
wisdom? Isn't he the son of Joseph the carpenter and Mary, whom

we all know?' From the traditional pictures of the holy family that
we have become accustomed to, one would imagine everybody
saying, 'I always knew there was something special about that
man, from the time he was a child. And with parents like Mary
and Joseph, how could he be otherwise?' But, no. From what they
had observed over the years, there was no obvious difference
between the family of Jesus and any other family of the town. In
other words, the ordinary home and family was good enough for
the Son of God. That fact must surely be an encouragement to
every family, however imperfect (and one's family is always
imperfect to its members).

Amenable, approachable

What sort of man was he? Sometimes he is depicted as distant,
awesome, a light shining out of him. In fact, he seems to have
been the most amenable and approachable of people. When John
the Baptist pointed out Jesus as the lamb of God to Andrew and
John, the eventual apostles, they followed him. He turned around
and asked 'What do you want?' They, presumably taken aback by
his abrupt and challenging question, said probably the first thing
that came into their heads, 'Where do you live?' 'Come and see',
he replied. However abrupt and challenging his original question,
there is no mistaking the warmth of his invitation to 'come and
see'. They spent the rest of the day with him. No doubt they
spoke together, but they also experienced him relaxed in his home.
Whatever happened, whatever was said, from that brief encounter
they became convinced that he was the Messiah, the anointed one
of God.

He mixed freely even with the most disreputable, to the horror of
respectable people – and who can blame them? The tax collectors
(whom to understand how despised and hated they were, think

'drug dealers' in today's world) and prostitutes felt totally at ease with him and he with them. Yet nobody could ever get the impression that he condoned their way of life. The sick and handicapped had no fear of approaching him, begging for healing.

His response to suffering tells us much about him, illustrated by the man suffering from leprosy (1) who said to him, 'If you want to, you can heal me,' to which Jesus responded, as if stung by the very suggestion that he might not want to heal him, 'Of course I want to' as he reached out and *touched* this man with the most contagious disease, and healed him. It was as if he could not bear to see somebody suffer, and so, responded in a way that was instinctive, impulsive, abundant, uncalculating. The power within him was used solely in order to heal.

No Concern for Himself

The temptations experienced by Jesus as described in the Gospels (2) may at first reading seem harmless enough. Many of us could think of more lurid and exotic temptations. In fact, they seek to touch him at the very heart of his mission, namely to use his power for his own benefit: to turn stones into bread to feed his hunger, to make a spectacular leap from the parapet of the temple, landing on his feet in order to impress the influential people in Jerusalem, to enjoy the good things of life that could be freely available to him. He would not hear of it. The power within him was used only for the healing of others and never for his own benefit, not even to promote his mission.

One detail of his temptations tells us much about the man Jesus. The first inclination on reading of the temptations is to imagine that he immediately brushed them aside, 'Get behind me, Satan'. But he spent forty days in the wilderness. During that time he pondered, he prayed, he agonised, he wrestled with temptation. Apparently it was not easy. But then he made his decision. He knew what he had to do. He set about preaching the kingdom of God on earth, challenging the world and its values.

Perhaps one of the qualities that have made him such an attractive personality through the centuries, even to people of no religious persuasion, was his lack of concern for himself: he sought nothing for himself, neither property nor wealth nor prestige nor popularity. This man was transparently authentic.

The Parables

He was in tune with the people and was able to speak to them in language they understood, using imaginative stories, the parables to make his point. The stories, like all the best stories always contain an element of surprise, and more than a touch of humour. One can imagine the twinkle in his eyes, a little smile, as he saw mouths open in amazement at the conclusion of his stories, when the lesson he was teaching had hit home.

The parables of the prodigal son, the good shepherd, the good Samaritan (the best known of all) are examples of his brilliance at using simple stories to illustrate a profound teaching – a quality that every preacher will envy. He was equally capable of dealing with the learned when they questioned him, either honestly seeking enlightenment or maliciously laying a trap for him.

Sometimes he uses wildly exaggerated images to make his point. Speaking of riches he says, 'It is easier for a camel to pass through the eye of a needle than for a rich man to enter heaven.'
'What right have you to point out the speck in your brother's eye, when you are not aware of the plank in your own eye!' 'If

somebody hits you on the right cheek, turn the other cheek!' Jesus himself, when struck across the cheek after his arrest, did not ask his persecutors to hit his other check – such bravado was not part of his make-up. This suggests that we do not give a pedantic, literal interpretation to such exaggerated statements when they are clearly making an emphatic point.

His Teaching

There was something beautiful about his teaching, a quality that would give heart to the most marginalised and down-trodden of people: blessed the poor in spirit, blessed the merciful, blessed the peacemakers. His listeners recognised his 'authority', not because of his exalted position, which he did not have, but from what they recognised as the truth of what he was saying. He turned upside-down so many of the values that motivate many people, not by ridiculing people's honest efforts to seek well-being, but by sketching out the alternative values, which are immediately seen to be so desirable.

We recognise what a better and happier world it would be if the values that Jesus taught were to become the norm, but sigh, 'if only' and tend to lay them gently aside while we get on with the real issues in the real world. A later chapter will endeavour to show how realistic, practical and sensible are the values that Jesus promotes.

Forgive us, as we too forgive!

Nothing singles out Jesus from all other great religious leaders as his teaching on forgiveness. Others speak of their confidence that God will forgive their sins. Jesus goes much further in a way that can only be called revolutionary. In the prayer he gave us, Jesus says, 'forgive us our trespasses, *as we forgive those who trespass against us*'(3). Not only believe that we receive forgiveness, but we too must give, must forgive. How basic this is to all he taught is shown in the prayer he gave us, the *Our* Father, where the only thing we undertake to do is to forgive. To forgive embraces all the other virtues he spoke about.

That is what makes Jesus different. *'Love your enemies, do good to those who hate you, bless those who curse you, pray for those who treat you badly'* .(4) As he hung on the cross, suffering physical and mental torments, Jesus was able to pray for those who inflicted such torture on him, *'Father, forgive them, for they know not what they do.'*(5)

It is noteworthy that, during the 'troubles' in Northern Ireland, there was no small number of heroic examples of forgiveness, and from both sides of the political divide. A family member was murdered. A parent, interviewed on national television, pleaded that there be no retaliation, no vengeance. To renounce the desire for revenge does not take away the hurt or the grief, which will always be there, but is the first and most important step towards forgiveness and eventual reconciliation.

Greatness through Serving

His other great teaching was illustrated by the example he gave after the last supper, when he washed the feet of his disciples (6) – to their horror, as this was a task, not for the master, but for the most junior of the family or servants. One can imagine arguments in families, 'I did it the last time. It is somebody else's turn now.' But Jesus was emphatic: 'If I, the Lord and Master, have washed your feet, you must wash each other's feet.'

He was even more explicit on the occasion that James and John came to him asking for seats at his right and left hand when he came into his kingdom, and the others were indignant with them for trying to steal a march on them. Jesus told them all that, while in the world *'the rulers lord it over them and great men make their authority felt. Among you this is not to happen. No; anyone who wants to become great among you must be your servant....., just as the Son of man came not to be served but to serve.'* (Matt. 20: 25-27).

Even those in positions of power seek, according to Jesus, not to dominate, but to serve the cause from the position they hold, with respect for those working for them, with them. There is nothing wrong with being the boss. Somebody has to be the manager and to guide whatever the operation is. But even from the top, the motive of service rather than domination is appropriate. At the other end of the social ladder, there is no such thing as a menial task, when it is carried out in a spirit of service. There is dignity in every task that is performed for the well-being of other individuals or of the community.

Be Generous

He tells us to be generous, with what we have and especially in our judgements. The only occasion when Jesus appears to speak with anger is when referring to those who pass judgement on others – whatever the appearances.

He told the story of the pharisee and the tax collector going up to the temple to pray. The pharisee recounted all his good works – and they were many – and thanked God he was not like that wretch at the back of the temple. That 'wretch' however, bowed his head, struck his breast and prayed for forgiveness –as, given his trade, he had every reason to. But Jesus concludes that the tax collector went home justified before God rather than the other, whose failure was to pass judgement and to look down on the sinner (7).

His own interaction with people, his desire to heal the sick and feed the hungry, is the best example of his teaching in practice.

Although gentle with the weak, he was strong when the need arose. While he respected authority, he was not overawed by the power of others. He spoke out as he saw fit, regardless of the risk he was taking of alienating those who could bring the weight of their authority down upon him.

When he spoke severely of those who imposed burdens on others and did nothing to help them bear them, some of the religious leaders realised only too well that he was referring to them. He himself was almost diffident in explaining to those who asked what their obligations were. The rich young man who came asking what he needed to do, was reminded, almost with a shrug of the shoulders of the commandments. When he insisted on more, that he wanted perfection, he was told in no uncertain terms what it implied – and that was not really what he wanted to hear. (8) He invited the first disciples to 'follow him'. It was an invitation rather than an order.

Jesus himself was open to all those who came to him for healing. He could not resist them, whether or not they were interested in his teachings. He used all his power to alleviate their suffering. He never condemned the weak, the sinner and, at the first sign of goodwill on their part, assured them of forgiveness. His words on the cross to the good thief, *'This day you shall be with me in paradise'* (9) must surely be the most consoling words ever spoken to a human being.

Son of God

What about his claim to be Son of God, which is most emphatically expressed in John's Gospel, but is the conclusion towards which the other versions of the Gospel draw the reader? In Matthew's account of the sermon on the mount, Jesus quotes the Word of God from the Old Testament, for example, *'Thou shalt not kill'* and follows it up saying *'but I say to you'* (10) and declares the more perfect way of not harbouring hatred or anger, thus daring to amend even the word of God. Each of the first three evangelists describes the transfiguration: *'his face shone like the sun and his clothes became as dazzling as light'*, Peter recalling the moment as one of total peace and fulfilment, a moment he would have wanted to hold forever. Then a voice from heaven was heard, *'This is my Son, my beloved. Listen to him.'* (11)
A short time previously Peter had acknowledged Jesus as *'the Christ, the Son of the living God.'* (Matt. 16:16). Matthew tells how the Roman centurion at the foot the cross, overwhelmed by the convulsions of nature that followed the death of Jesus, exclaimed *'In truth this man was Son of God.'*

John, writing much later than the other evangelists and presuming his readers were familiar with them, is uncompromising from the first words of his Gospel: *'In the beginning was the Word...the Word was God...the Word was made flesh and dwelt among us.'* John starts from the assumption that Jesus is the Son of God and places a selected number of events in the life of Jesus in that context. Jesus emphatically claims that he and the Father are one. He states *'I am the good shepherd'*, *'I am the light of the world'*, *'I am the Way, the Truth, the Life'* (12). Who else could make such claims? A preacher or teacher might say 'I can show you the way; I can teach you the truth,' but 'I AM the Way, I AM the Truth, I AM the Life' can only be said by one who is very sure of his oneness with God the

Father. John's readers would make the connection with God's manifestation to Moses, when God, asked by Moses who He was, gave His name as *'I am.'* (Exodus 3:14).

The authorities who connived at his death recognised the implications of all that he said. The question has been asked, Would they have put to death somebody who merely preached an attractive message of love of neighbour? They obviously recognised another dimension to this man. *'No one would crucify a teacher who told pleasant stories to enforce prudential morality.'*(13)

Our scientific age looks for proof: 'How do you prove that Jesus is God made man?' It cannot be proved scientifically because it does not fall within the remit of science. One can point to the authenticity of the man, illustrated by his total unselfishness, to the nobility of his teaching, to the power he exercised over sickness, over demons, over the elements, etc. and to the authority of his teaching. Ultimately, however, one must make a leap of faith, uniting oneself in a holy communion with this man, and with what such a union implies. Such a leap of faith is not irrational. On the contrary, it is a perfectly reasonable conclusion to draw from what each one of the evangelists tells us in his different way.

Extraordinary Things

Some scholars devote their lives to the study of scripture. We owe them a great debt of gratitude. By filling in the background to the different books of scripture, by teasing out the original meaning of words in the language of the original text, by studying the literary forms that were employed in narrative at different periods, and so much else, they enrich our understanding. They also put us at ease regarding questions we might puzzle over and be uneasy about.

There are some marvels described in the life of Jesus from the moment of his conception to the end of his life on earth. The events surrounding his birth – the angels, the shepherds, the wise men, the gifts – can alienate some. The modern mind has been influenced by the scientific method, which looks for precision and accuracy, and rightly so. Precision and accuracy are the tools of scripture scholars too. But the modern mind is in danger of missing the poetry of a story. Luke's narrative of the nativity is a beautiful story, conveying with the gentle and poetic subtlety of an artist that this child was destined by God for something extraordinary.

This subtlety is typical of the synoptic writers, who suggest comparisons with prophecies for example, rather than spelling out facts as 'proof'. The events of the life of Jesus are left to speak for themselves. We readers are left to draw our own conclusions. John's Gospel is more explicit.

Great volumes are written on the Gospels. No other books have been subjected to such scrutiny over the centuries, usually honestly searching for truth, sometimes endeavouring to disprove and debunk. They have stood the test of time, and of the most critical examination.

2000 plus Years On

Is it not extraordinary that a life that ended with failure and disgrace in the crucifixion, should suddenly be alive again, attracting countless numbers of followers in a very short time, and ever since?

Is it not extraordinary that over 2000 years later, the birth of Jesus is celebrated as a festival throughout the world each year, and Christians flock to their churches to mark the occasion, as countless millions have done throughout those 2000 years? The abuse of Christ's name to justify violence and persecution, as it has been used disgracefully, from time to time is far outweighed by the goodness of so many Christians, their works of mercy, the heroic service of many consecrated souls to the sick, the eagerness to evangelise, to spread the Good News. Jesus has been an inspiration to countless numbers of people during all that time, not only the heroic but also those who count themselves 'ordinary', who look to Jesus as the guiding star of their lives. That is true today as it has been for the past 2000 years.

All things considered, one is happy to exclaim with the Roman centurion, 'In truth this man was the Son of God.'(14) He is indeed the Way, the Truth, the Life.

1. Matt.8:2-4; Mark 1:40-46; Luke 5:12-14.
2. Matt.4:1-11; Mark 1:12-13; Luke 4:1-13
3. Matt.7:12; Luke 6:31
4. Matt. 5:43-47; Luke 6:27,28
5. Luke 23:34
6. John 13:3-11
7. Luke 18:9-14
8. Matt.19:16-22; Mark 10:17-22; Luke 18:18-23
9. Luke 23:39-43
10. Matt.5:21,22. See also verses 27,31,33,39,44.
11. Matt.17:1-8; Mark 9:2-8; Luke 9:28-36
12. John 10;1-8; 8:12; 14:6
13. CWE Smith, *The Jesus of the Parables*, quoted by Pope Benedict XVI in *Jesus of Nazareth*, p.186.
14. Matt.27:54

4. THE GOSPEL MAKES SENSE

The Gospel might be seen as a beautiful and idealistic way of life, but unrealistic in the hard world of economics, of business, of competition for promotion, of international relations.

Peace and Reconciliation

On the other hand, since the 1939-45 war, the nations of Europe have gradually come together, beginning with France and Germany coming to an agreement which would ensure that there would never again be war between them over the coal and iron mines on the border between them. Gradually, the spirit of this agreement led to other nations of Europe joining in what is now the European Union, consisting of 25 nations. Being a human institution it has its faults, but it does make it inconceivable that war would break out again between the nations of Western Europe. There is now a forum for resolving difficult questions, without having recourse to violence.

Furthermore the European Union has a fund which is distributed to the poorer countries to enable them establish an infrastructure on which to build towards greater prosperity, a system which operates to great effect. The sharing out of resources of the wealthier nations among the poorer is surely an example of the spirit of the Gospel in practice. The hard-headed representatives of the richer countries recognise that, ultimately it is in their interests too. As the Pope is continually pointing out, the way of justice is the way to peace.

On a wider level, the United Nations endeavours to be a forum for all the nations of the world, to enable them resolve differences in a peaceful manner. It does not always succeed, but the forum is there, however imperfect. The United Nations has promulgated a Declaration of Human Rights, which it proposes as the norm for all people. There are many instances of the violation of such rights, but the objective is there for all to see, and to recognise violations as such.

Under the umbrella of the United Nations, there are various bodies, e.g. to promote the welfare of children, to come to the aid of famine-stricken people, to promote art and culture, there is an army of peacekeepers, soldiers volunteered by member nations to preserve peace between hostile factions.

In both institutions the spirit of the Gospel is at work, whether or not it is invoked explicitly. *'Blessed the peacemakers; they shall be called sons of God.'* The spirit of both the European Union and of the United Nations is that there is a better way of resolving disputes than by violence, and that justice is an unavoidable pathway on the road to peace. Centuries of a culture based on Gospel values are not easily shaken off, even when those values are frequently dishonoured, and the influence remains – because it makes sense.

The Gospel tells us that the response to violence is not further violence, which has a way of spiralling out of control, but rather to seek reconciliation. Seeking reconciliation is not a soft option. It means swallowing one's pride, disregarding the taunts of others who cry for revenge. Reconciliation is not appeasement, is not yielding supinely to unreasonable or unjust demands for the sake of a quiet life. It seeks to find the cause for anger and then endeavours to deal with the hurt. Often the interests of a few can lead to injustice and oppression, which eventually explodes in violence. Reconciliation will first endeavour to put right the injustice, to relieve those who are oppressed.

Vengeance is not a matter of honour, but of weakness posing as strength, especially when it leads to the slaughter of countless innocent people. *'Love your enemies, do good to those who hate you, bless those who curse you, pray for those who treat you badly.'* (Luke 6:27,28)

There are times when policing has no option but to use a minimum of violence to subdue an aggressor. The operative word is 'minimum'. The problem is that once the demon of violence is unleashed, it is difficult to restrain it again, until one or both combatants collapse exhausted. Then negotiation takes place. If only the negotiation had taken place sooner or even in the beginning! If only the powers in the Middle East, in Iraq, in Afghanistan, not to mention the US and the UK, had approached their task determined ultimately to seek reconciliation, so many lives would have been spared, so much suffering avoided and people would have been enabled to pursue their lives in peace.

But it is not simple. Sometimes politicians are faced with making agonising decisions, which they know might lead to great suffering but which seem necessary to achieve ultimate peace and stability. The EU and the UN are proof that cooperation, building up the weak, liberating the oppressed, seeking the path of reconciliation not only works, but works for the betterment of everybody concerned.

What is true between nations is true also in families and in personal relationships. It is sad when members of a family fall out and do not speak for years, because nobody has the strength to make an approach and to seek reconciliation. It can happen that when somebody has the courage to take the initiative and helps re-build the bridge of relationship between the angry parties, that the effort is greeted with relief by everybody concerned. A situation is relieved that, in their hearts nobody really wanted.

Seeking revenge is a destructive force in one's life. Nourishing resentment is like a poison that destroys one's inner peace. It does not harm the one against whom it is directed but it most surely destroys the one in whom it simmers unchecked. It is important to distinguish between feeling the pain of past hurts and seeking revenge. If one can truthfully say that one is not seeking revenge, not seeking to return hurt for hurt, then one can truthfully say that one has forgiven – even though the pain, the hurt is still there and surfaces when one is reminded of the past. Not to seek revenge is the first and most important step on the way to forgiveness and forgiveness is the way to peace of heart.

Greatness through Serving

Jesus tells us emphatically that greatness is achieved, not by dominating others, but by serving them. Imagine a country where *'Love your neighbour as yourself'* became the guiding norm for the government. Imagine a political party that took that magnificent ideal as its manifesto!

While having to cope with the demands of the free market, of the economy, with the problems of law and crime, the guiding principle would be the well-being of the people. The measure of progress would be the improving lot of the people rather than the percentage rise in the growth of the economy, though the two are not incompatible. It is a matter of priorities.

A major function of the government would be to protect and sustain the weak and the sick. The government, leading by example would promote a spirit of service in the country.

It must be said that the spirit of the National Health Service and of Social Security is precisely that, to ensure that the sick have the best medical care, regardless of ability to pay, and that those who are poor for any reason, are enabled to live lives of at least basic dignity. Everybody is given the opportunity of education, at least to the end of secondary level.

Tightening of support for general health, social services and education coexists with a relatively small number of people being paid enormous sums of money as salaries and bonuses, annual salaries greater than a nurse or a teacher would be paid in a lifetime. The priorities need to be frequently re-stated, the star of the nation's ideals kept clearly in view.

Unfortunately, in the world evil exists in a real way, in real people motivated by greed for more and more wealth and possessions; by a lust for power, to be the boss and to dominate others, to create a personal empire; by a hunger for self-indulgence, feasting, binge drinking, engaging in casual sex without love, without commitment.

Unfortunately too, such people tend to have influence disproportionately to their numbers, a loud voice that drowns out those who may object. They can also be very persuasive and very clever. Jesus said of the unjust steward *'The children of this world are wiser in their own generation than the children of light.'* (Luke 16;8) Those who lust for power and achieve it are in a position to make or to influence decisions that affect everybody, but which are directed towards self-interest of the few. Their lavish life-style can appeal to others and attract imitation as the way to success. Those who live a life of self-indulgence describe themselves as 'having a good time'.

There is nothing wrong with ambition. On the contrary, Jesus tells the story of the talents, where those who use their talents to gain more are praised, while the one who buries his talent is condemned. Nor is there anything wrong with enjoying the good things of life. There is nothing virtuous about being miserable.

Common to all evil attitudes and action is putting self first, with disregard for the well-being of others. Other people are used. Those who get in the way are liable to be trampled underfoot. Everything about an evil way of life is the antithesis of 'Love your neighbour as yourself.'

The most challenging Gospel passage is the story in chapter 25 of Matthew's Gospel of the king passing judgement on his people, separating them like sheep and goats on his right and left. His criterion was whether they fed the hungry, visited the sick or those in prison, clothed the naked etc., for *'as often as did it (or did it not) to one of these my least ones, you did it (or did it not) to me.'* Jesus identifying himself in this personal and intimate way with the most down-trodden and deprived is both challenging and acutely uncomfortable – but also magnificent.

The human spirit resonates with the spirit of the Gospel. John F Kennedy in his inaugural address as President of the USA in 1961 inspired a generation of young and old when he proclaimed *'Ask not what your country can do for you, ask rather what you can do for your country.'* When men or women die, what is remembered and celebrated is, not the amount of money they had or how much power they exerted or how they had indulged themselves, but rather to what extent they had benefited their fellow human beings. *'Anyone who wants to be great among you must be your servant,'* (Mark 10:43; see also Matt 20:24-28, Luke 22:24-27) i.e. not a servant in the grovelling sense but someone dedicated to promoting the welfare of others.

There is nobody so miserable and to be pitied as the selfish person, the rich man feasting sumptuously so absorbed in himself that he did not even notice the poor man at his feet, starving and covered in sores. (Luke 16:19-31) Such people are never content. They think only of themselves, are indifferent to the needs of others and lack the basic quality needed for a healthy relationship, namely the ability to love.

Human beings are social animals who, for their own fulfilment and happiness need to be able to interact with their fellow humans. But it has got to be on the basis of mutual respect and concern. Mother Teresa tells of a woman who came pleading for food because she was destitute and her children were hungry. Having received a bountiful supply of food, she said as she expressed her gratitude, 'Now I shall be able to give some to my friend who is in a similar plight to me.' The dignity and nobility of a generous person is clear for all to see – and such people always seem to be so happy, at peace within themselves.

Simplicity of Life

For many years, with the development of technology, we have been able to plunder our planet and draw extravagantly on its resources to improve our quality of life. Coal, oil, natural gas is extracted in enormous quantities, the land is tilled twice or three times a year, forests are cut down, oceans are brutally plundered until even the fish can no longer keep up with demand. The delicate balance of our bounteous and beautiful and usually resilient planet has been upset. Not only are irreplaceable resources of the planet diminishing, but the volume of emissions from the burning of fuels and from other sources is threatening the future of our very existence on this earth.

And all for the sake of 'More'. 'More' has been the watchword of the consumer society. It expresses the insatiable appetite of the late twentieth century. It is like the idols venerated by primitive societies – the great god MORE must be satisfied by endless sacrifices.

Now, we are beginning to reap the consequences – collapse of the world economic system in 2008, unpredictable climate changes. In a more primitive age, such consequences would be attributed to an angry God punishing His people for their greed. We know however, that it is we ourselves who have brought these situations about and it is we who must find a response.

In the Sermon on the Mount, Jesus says: *'I am telling you not to worry about your life and what you are to eat, nor about your body and what you are to wear. Surely life is more than food, and the body more than clothing!'* etc. (Matt.7:25). His own way of life was a life of utter simplicity. However, it was not a life of misery. Jesus enjoyed company, enjoyed celebrating a meal with others, whether of the outcasts or of the learned and wealthy.

The word that would express his advice to us is ENOUGH, as distinct from 'more'. For the sake of our future and especially that of our children and grandchildren, we must learn to say at the end of each day, in the spirit of the Gospel: 'Thank God I had enough today.'

People of Hope

It has been pointed out that the difference between the poverty of the 1930s and the poverty of the 21st century is that then people lived lives of dignity even in their poverty, endeavouring to encourage their children, through education, to aspire to something greater and often making considerable sacrifices to enable them do so. That still happens, of course – generalisations are always dangerous. But there is a poverty of spirit now that expresses itself in vandalism, in ugly and crude graffiti, in a cult of ugliness, in recourse to addictive drugs of all sorts, leading to crime and violence. Hope, and the lack of it is the difference between the two.

Hope is not an airy optimism, saying 'don't worry; everything will be alright', founded on nothing more than a desire to feel good or to console. Hope is well-founded. It is the great Jewish virtue, shown in their history, persecuted and driven out (often sadly by Christians) but always convinced that God was with them and would achieve His great purpose through them.

For the Christian, hope is based on Christ crucified and risen from the dead. The cross is the most powerful religious symbol. It tells of love. Can our imagination cope with the idea of all the evil that ever has been and ever will be committed by us human beings, but being counteracted by an act of love so great that it is greater, more immense than all the evil put together? That is the power of Christ, Son of God who shed his blood on the cross for the forgiveness of sins.

Then Christ rose from the dead. However we explain it, Christ is a living and powerful influence, an inspiration for countless millions of people today as he has been throughout all the centuries since his lifetime. Christ overcame, not only death, but also the forces of evil that crucified an innocent man, overcame evil not only for himself but for all people, for all time.

The most frightening possibility is that ultimately, the forces of evil will prevail. The Resurrection of Christ is our guarantee that it will not happen. *'The gates of hell shall not prevail'* Jesus had assured Peter and the apostles (Matt. 16:18). Hence, Christians have a firm, well-founded belief that the good in human beings is more widespread, a more powerful, more enduring force than is their tendency to evil.

This hope has been borne out in history. Evil empires bear within themselves the seeds of their own destruction. Even at times of greatest despair, charismatic figures arise pointing to a better way of life, carrying with them the multitudes who aspire to simple peace and goodness in their lives for themselves and their families.

The Christian also firmly believes in life in the world to come. What it consists of is hard to imagine, though it does exercise the imagination of some visionaries. This belief follows from Jesus risen from the dead, Jesus alive and real among us even now. It does not take from the importance of the present moment, but rather enhances it. The present is a step on a great journey that ends with God in all His reality, glory and fullness.

'We wait in joyful hope for the coming of our Saviour Jesus Christ.'

5. THE CHURCH

Jesus did not establish an institution. The institution arose
from necessity, once groups of people began to come together.
Where two or three come together for a common purpose there
you have an institution. Hence, the Church as an institution came
into being.

Little groups used to gather in each other's houses to reflect
together on Scripture and to 'break bread together', i.e. to
celebrate the Eucharist. As these groups multiplied there was a
need for cohesion and guidance. When Paul, on his missionary
journeys, had baptised and confirmed a sizeable group in a
particular town, he appointed elders to lead the local Church, and
then moved on to the next town. (In parenthesis it might be noted
that Paul entrusted the Church to a group who had only recently
been baptised. It puts into proportion the present-day
lamentation about the 'shortage' of priests.)

Paul wrote his several letters, usually in response to queries from
local Churches which he had established, asking for clarification,
and sometimes to chastise them– in his inimitable and forthright
way - for misbehaviour he had heard about. When controversial
issues arose, the apostles assembled in Jerusalem to make a
decision and their authority was accepted.

It was the emperor Constantine who in the 5th century, having
been converted to Christianity, took the Church under his wing.
To some extent, the Church became a respectable institution. The
ragged and hounded group with their revolutionary notions of
cherishing the outcasts and of making peace with the enemy,
became domesticated.

The 'hierarchy' of bishop, priest, lay people took shape, the norms and vestments for the celebration of the Sacraments were created, and an era began when magnificent churches and basilicas were built. Sacred music was gradually composed, ranging from the austere simplicity and reverence of plainsong to the grandiose Masses created by the great composers, such as Mozart and Beethoven.

Artists and architects used their creative talents and skills to express their faith, bequeathing works of great beauty and magnificence to succeeding generations. Stone masons patiently chipped at hard stone to create an image or a decoration, which would be lifted high up into the cathedral as it was being built, to be visible only to the One who sees all. The art, the beautiful and awesome buildings testify to generations of faith, who were convinced that only the best they could offer was good enough for God.

It is all a far cry from the simplicity of the Master, who *'had not where to lay his head'*(1). Nevertheless, there is a solidity and permanence about the structure of the Church, which ensures continuity and facilitates many things that individuals could not accomplish alone. It cannot be denied that a solemn celebration of the liturgy in a grand church is a beautiful and uplifting experience.

The reality of the Church is best experienced in the people who come together on Sunday for Mass, to hear the Word of Scripture and to partake of the Eucharist. They are the faithful people of God, who as they look around on Sunday recognise others who have the same beliefs and priorities as themselves. Their very presence is an encouragement and support to each other. They do not make claims to be better than others, because they know how they have to struggle to lead a good life, and are conscious that they do not always succeed in every detail. They bring with them their preoccupations, their pain, their hopes and aspirations, and go out, nourished and strengthened for the week ahead. They endeavour to live by the values they believe in, at work, in their families. Many of them engage in catechesis, in social work, in fund-raising, in visiting sick and housebound people.

Authority

The 'authority' of Church teaching is the subject of much discussion. The clue for the meaning of such authority is found in the Gospel. *'The teaching of Jesus made a deep impression on the people because he taught them with authority, unlike their own scribes'* (2)

The source of the authority of Jesus came not from his office: he had no office; not from a uniform he was wearing: he did not wear a uniform. His authority came from his listeners recognising the truth and the nobility of what he was preaching.(3)

That is the sort of authority that the Church seeks to exercise. In dealing with issues, whether controversial or elaborating some application of the Gospel in a contemporary context, the Catholic Church sets out its arguments in great detail. It is not satisfied with saying 'The Church teaches, and therefore everybody must obey,' though some of its local leaders tend sometimes to do so. It is true that many are happy to accept a teaching because the Church says so, without getting too involved with the why and wherefore, content to accept the principles involved, in a way not all that different from how they accept the judgement of a doctor or a teacher. The Church takes a long-term view of issues, looking beyond individual needs to the ultimate effect of a particular course of action. Its authority stems from people recognising the truth and nobility of the stand it takes, even when that stance is deeply unpopular and demanding.

Infallibility is, frankly an uncomfortable issue. The First Vatican Council declared in 1870 that the Pope is infallible when he pronounces on matters of faith and morals. In fact, the only occasion since then when the Pope has invoked infallibility has been the Assumption of Our Lady into heaven, which cannot be described as an earth-shattering issue. There were occasions when it seemed that Pope John Paul II felt so strongly that he would make an infallible declaration, but he did not.

If ever there was an occasion for declaring infallible, surely it was when the documents of the Second Vatican Council were published, bearing as they did the approval of all the assembled bishops of the world and of the Pope. But Pope John XXIII had stated explicitly from the beginning that the tone of the Council would be pastoral rather than dogmatic. In practical terms, it seems infallibility is a non-issue.

One wonders whether the very notion of infallibility has inhibited the Church from invoking it, because afterwards there is no turning back, there is no scope for development or growth in understanding. More worryingly, the notion of infallibility leads to an attitude of 'We cannot be wrong;' which gradually becomes 'We cannot do wrong', leading to disastrous consequences.

Even at a lower level of *magisterium* there is a fear of amending past statements lest the authority of the Church be shaken. Such fear is unworthy of the Church of Christ. Human knowledge grows, human sensitivities develop, sometimes clarifying an aspect of a question that was not recognised in the past. In all teaching and preaching, the one imperative is the truth.

There are, of course unshakeable principles, whatever world developments or discoveries may take place. But there is also freedom in being able to embrace progress in any field of knowledge or skills and to see it in the light of the Gospel. The criterion of progress always is whether it contributes to the well-being of the human race, not just a few powerful individuals. (4) We look to the teaching Church to distinguish between principle and progress, when we find it difficult to do so ourselves.

When Jesus commissioned the eleven disciples to go out and preach to all the nations he promised *'I am with you always, to the close of the age'* (Matt. 28:20). His Spirit would always be with his Church, to guide and direct it. There is no need to fret about the positioning of commas or the precise wording of a dogmatic statement or even to expect simple answers, any answers to complicated questions. (5) God's Spirit will inspire, will direct, will correct when mistakes are made, will keep the barque of Peter on course through the storms and turbulence that is inevitable. How many times did Jesus say to his disciples *'Do not be afraid'*!

The compassionate face of Christ in the World

The criterion for the authenticity of the Church is whether it reflects the compassionate face of Christ in its care for the poor, the sick, the rejects of society. Religious congregations and societies through the centuries have provided education, health care and homes for those who would otherwise have been without. They still do, though in the more developed countries these services have been taken over by the state. For that reason, many congregations established to meet a particular need are likely to disappear. However, the history of the Church is the story of charismatic individuals who emerge from time to time, recognise a great need in society or in the Church and set up a structure to deal with it. In modern times, Mother Teresa, Jean Vanier, Brother Roger of Taize are examples of what is suggested. Furthermore, many lay organizations, attached to or loosely connected with the Church continue the works of mercy, for example in famine relief, human development and human rights.

The Christ of the Gospels was never judgemental of human frailty, though always gently conveying that he did not condone the sin. The word 'condemn' is not part of the Gospel vocabulary, though it is a word beloved of headline writers in conveying what the Church is teaching. The only time Jesus uses strong language is towards those who pass judgement on others, those who lay heavy burdens on others but will not lift a finger in support.

Divisions

In the past, much damage has been done to the credibility of Christianity by the divisions that occurred in the sixteenth century. Different churches broke away from Rome because of dissatisfaction or disagreement, leading to bitter polemic designed to prove that 'We are right and you are wrong.' The unchristian bitterness and refusal to interact lasted for centuries, was indeed a scandal and, where it still exists remains so.

In the Catholic Church, the Second Vatican Council of 1962-65 brought about a profound change in the attitudes of the Catholic people in this regard, (6) a change to which other churches, for the most part have responded generously. The notion of division has been replaced by diversity. Where division led to argument and hostility, diversity is seen as enrichment, which enables different churches learn from each other.

The Catholic Church has learned a great deal about Scripture and the celebration of the Word from other churches for whom Scripture has always been paramount. The lectern for the proclamation of the Word is given a central place in their churches and chapels. Their scholars produced great works to enable readers of the Bible do so with fuller understanding. Only in the twentieth century did Catholic scholars enter this field in a big way, and they inherited the scholarship of previous centuries from other churches. Now Scripture scholarship flourishes in the Catholic Church and the Liturgy of the Word occupies a prominent place in the Mass. Prayerful reflection on Scripture in groups is growing (known as *lectio divina*).

Catholics have also inherited the rich hymnody of the other churches. A typical hymnal in use in Catholic churches will contain hymns once regarded as 'Protestant', which priests and people sing quite happily, without fear of being denounced as heretics.

On the other hand, the Catholic Church has made its own contribution to the common enrichment of Christian churches. It has produced many mystics and spiritual writers, from whom other churches often draw with profit. The Catholic emphasis on the Eucharist has been taken up by other churches, many of which have renewed their celebration of the Eucharist.

The Eucharist

The assembly of people of faith to worship God, as they know Him, has been likened to children at play. It is when children are at play that they are most themselves. There is no serious purpose to what they are doing, there is no product, they are relaxed and rejoice in being together.

The Mass is the gathering of Catholic people to worship God. It is a relaxed, non-competitive, non-productive assembly. Being there is sufficient explanation for their presence. The simple fact of coming together in a group, large or small, expresses something difficult to put into words, recognises God with us, among us, within us.

The Eucharist is described as the 'sign of our unity'. Sadly, for the Catholic Church in relation to the others it is the sign of our disunity. All churches who celebrate the Eucharist believe that Christ is present in the bread and wine consecrated by an ordained minister. A columnist in one of the quality newspapers commented on one occasion, 'People who believe that will believe anything!' That comment shows the sad ignorance of an intelligent man.

We believe Christ is present in the bread and wine of the Eucharist because he said so. That is how he would make himself present for his people for all time, so that they could unite themselves most intimately with him. It would be hard to think of a more imaginative way of expressing unity: the bread and wine of the Eucharist are absorbed into the body and become part of the recipient, giving life and energy, i.e. Christ is absorbed into the recipient and becomes part of that person's very self, expressed by St Paul as *'I live now, not I, but Christ lives in me,'* (7). One's individuality is not diminished thereby but rather enhanced and enriched. Absorption in Christ is truly described as a holy com-union. This is the faith of all Christian churches which celebrate the Eucharist.

One imagines an astronaut circling our planet on a Sunday, tuned in to the sounds coming from the earth and hearing throughout the day as he passes different time-zones the same words from every latitude and longitude: 'he took, he blessed, he broke, he gave .... this is my body'. The celebration of the Eucharist is a summary and expression of the whole Christian life. It explains who Jesus was, what he meant and what he means.

Problems arise when we endeavour to rationalise the manner of Christ's presence, and when we get entangled in the vexed question of the validity of the ordination of ministers. These are sensitive questions that do not surface greatly in these days of improving relationships. However, a Catholic taking part in a service in another church which includes celebration of the Eucharist may be the only person who does not go forward for Holy Communion. It feels wrong. In every other way the Catholic is in harmony with all the prayers, the readings, the whole thrust of the service. One might say 'in communion with'. May not goodwill and honest faith count for more in the sight of God than the intricacies of theology – important though theology is? There is encouragement, but no solution in the heart-felt quote from Pope John Paul II's encyclical on Christian Unity: ' ... *we do have a burning desire to join in celebrating the one Eucharist of the Lord, and this desire itself is already a common prayer of praise.'* (8)

In the previous chapter we reflected on the love of Christ expressed by shedding his blood for the forgiveness of sins, and how that act of love is greater than all evil, past or future. That act of love is on-going, expressed again and again when Christians gather to fulfil Christ's will to 'do this in memory of me'. The proclamation of the mysteries of our faith is our response to the consecration of the bread and wine: 'Christ has died; Christ is risen; Christ will come again.'

The sharing of a meal is a human and instinctive way of expressing and celebrating friendship, from the child offering a dive into the bag of crisps to the adult inviting friends to dinner, or offering a cup of tea to a visitor. The unity and friendship of the shared meal is expressed in holy communion, where all present partake of the bread and the wine of the Eucharist, the body and blood of Christ, thereby expressing their union with each other, in Christ. The Acts of the Apostles, describing the early church after the time of Christ, speak of the people coming together in each other's houses for *'the breaking of bread'*, (9) breaking in order to share the one bread, the body of Christ.

It is a powerful moment when the congregation make their way in procession, with background music or, just as impressively in silence, to be offered the bread and the wine of the Eucharist: *The Body of Christ, Amen; the Blood of Christ, Amen.* Amen, amen, yes I believe it is the Body of Christ, it is the Blood of Christ.

For Catholics, the reality of Christ's presence in the Eucharist has always been a vital element of their faith. The consecrated bread, the Body of Christ, is reserved in the tabernacle, signalled by the warm glow of a red lamp, and is the centre of devotion. Sometimes it is exposed in a monstrance, before which the people pray with great reverence. The candles and lights that surround it create an atmosphere of warmth and intimacy, conducive to prayer.

It is a great loss in modern times that most churches are kept closed outside of times for services, for fear of vandalism and desecration. People are thus deprived of the grace of brief prayerful visits that sanctify their activities as they go about their daily duties. Where there's a will, there's a way, says the old proverb and no doubt there is a way here too, as some priests have found, if there is the will.

Controversial Questions

In modern times, the Catholic Church has found itself taking a strong and highly unpopular line on liberal laws inspired by individual anguish. The Church takes a long-term view of the consequences of crossing clearly demarcated lines. Unfortunately, its stance is often reported in news media in negative terms, the Church 'condemning'. The stance of the Church is not of condemning anybody, but rather protecting the sanctity of marriage vows and of human life.

It recognises that the welfare of society depends on the health and well-being of the family, that is family normally of man, woman and child or children. It is a tragedy for everybody concerned when a family breaks up, often after years of unhappiness and, on occasions even of violence. When it happens, the trauma suffered by the children is only beginning to be recognised. Some of them experience severe emotional problems as they grow up, sometimes leading to drug-taking, crime and homelessness. The scale on which it is happening is an example of a line being crossed, i.e. the marriage vows being set aside, and once that is accepted there is no line beyond. What was originally a compassionate response to a difficult case eventually becomes common practice. One dares to suggest that the scale of family breakdown is the greatest social problem of our age.

There are, of course, many cases where a spouse, having suffered bitterly in an unhappy marriage, divorces and finds peace and happiness in a second marriage, endeavouring to bring up the children in the best possible way, taking them to church, preparing them for the Sacraments. The present official practice is to exclude them from Holy Communion for all time. Surely there must be a better way. The argument is that if they were allowed Holy Communion this would give the impression that the Church now condones divorce and setting aside the marriage vows. It is not good enough for an individual priest to tell them quietly to receive Holy Communion, as long as nobody notices! Subterfuge is no way for the Church of Christ to resolve a problem. There is undoubtedly a dilemma, though Jesus never seemed to worry about what false impression people might get.

There is no simple solution. Those who suffer anguish through being deprived of holy communion might accept the position as their recognition, indeed their statement that the marriage vows are sacred. The desire for holy communion is itself a profound prayer. Sometimes all we can say is, 'Lord, I am doing my best. Please make up for me what I am missing.'

The other great issue where the Church takes a strong stand is on the sanctity of human life. This is a positive stance. It is not merely being opposed to abortion and euthanasia. It recognises that life is the most basic of human rights, that it is the sacred right of every human being from the moment of conception, through birth, youth, adulthood, old age, in sickness and in health.

To legalise the taking of life at any stage is to cross a line beyond which there is no further line of restraint. The practice of abortion is a perfect example: originally legalised under stringent conditions, but once allowed, the conditions became more and more liberal. The present situation of abortion virtually on demand, where sometimes pregnant girls are pressurised by family and friends to 'get rid of it', alarms even those who campaigned to have it legalised in the first place. Perhaps those who argue for legal euthanasia should take note.

There is a not too often quoted footnote to the Church's declaration on procured abortion: *This declaration expressly leaves aside the question of the moment when the spiritual soul is infused.*(10) It recognises diversity of opinion, some arguing for the first instant of conception, others stating that it could not precede nidation, or implantation in the womb. However, the footnote continues that a belated animation still recognises a human life calling for a soul from the moment of conception, and, in either case, the probable existence of the soul makes the taking of the life involve the risk of killing a human being.

It is worth noting that the argument for human life from the first moment of conception comes not from a Church pronouncement, but from the progress of bio-technology which can identify many characteristics of the person from the moment of union of sperm and ovum. In arguing for respect for human life from the moment of conception, the Church is doing no more than recognising what modern science is saying. However, during approximately fourteen days between conception and nidation in the womb, abortion occurs naturally on a considerable scale. During this period too, the embryo occasionally splits thus creating identical twins. Do these facts suggest a grey area for further reflection and discussion? Dare one say it?

There are often difficult situations in life and there are different ways of dealing with them. The most drastic solutions are not necessarily the best. Human enterprise, ingenuity and generosity usually finds a way.

The Church in the World

The Church has been described as the People of God, the visible sign of the kingdom of heaven among us. St Paul uses the image of the human body of which Christ is the head, all the members combining for the well-being of the whole body (11). He could not have known what a brilliant image it is. Modern science tells of the countless cells that make up the human body, each one an individual working for the well-being of the whole body.

Whatever the image, the people who are the Church are Christ's presence in the world, however imperfect and inadequate they may feel. Their efforts to be thoroughly Christian in all circumstances are a sign to the world. Just as the steeple of the traditional church is like a finger pointing upwards, reminding a busy city centre of a greater reality than their business, so the efforts of a Christian to be honest and trustworthy, to be generous and thoughtful even in the toughest and most competitive work, is a sign of Christ's presence in the secular world.

1. Matthew 8:20, Luke 9:58
2. Matthew 7: 28,29
3. See chapter on 'Jesus'
4. John Paul II Encyclical *Redemptor Hominis* n.16. See also Pope Benedict XVI's social encyclical 'Caritas in Veritate'.
5. See final chapter on 'Difficult Questions'
6. See Vatican Council decree on Ecumenism *Unitatis Redintegratio.*
7. Galatians 2:20.
8. Encyclical *Ut Unum Sint,* n.45
9. Acts of the Apostles, 2:46
10. footnote n.20 Declaration by the Sacred Congregation for the Doctrine of the Faith on Procured Abortion, 1974.
11. Romans 12:4,5; 1 Corinthians 12:12-31; Colossians 1;18 etc.

6. RITUAL

'The Mass is boring!' How that teenage judgement must pierce the heart of every priest. One thing is certain: The Mass is not boring. It is some of those present who are bored. Whose fault is it? Is it the priest's? Or can it be dismissed with a shrug of the shoulders 'Youngsters nowadays ...... '?

Looking for scapegoats is futile. Priest and people can only do their best. Some will respond. Some will not. This chapter is a reflection on what it might mean to 'do our best'.

There are well-established rituals for all sorts of special occasions, such as a wedding, a funeral, graduation at universities, the state opening of parliament. Special vestments are worn, those attending wear their best formal clothes, there are processions, speeches etc. It is an instinctive way of conveying the solemn nature of the event. Rehearsals take place beforehand to ensure that every detail of the ceremonial is carried out correctly and with dignity.

The Mass

While the events already mentioned take place only at rare intervals, the Mass takes place every day, with special emphasis on Sunday. The ritual is always the same, the only changeable part being the readings of scripture. There is a real danger that the recitation of the words, the same words, the performance of the actions, the same actions, becomes so familiar that they can be performed almost without thinking, with little or no preparation.

The Sunday Mass is a wonderful occasion. All those people have made the effort to be present, because they want to be there. Some

of them will have made a special effort, the elderly struggling
breathlessly along the road, but they would not miss it; parents
with several children of various ages, having organised the family
and bringing them along, perhaps feeling drained as a result;
teenagers, and indeed others braving the sneering comments of
some of their peers; some may have been tempted to take a rest
today but managed to get themselves there. All this effort is in
itself a great expression of faith, worth remarking from time to
time. The celebration of its liturgy, when the community comes
together to pray and worship is when the Church expresses its
very essence.

The Mass is an expression of a community with something
precious in common – all these people share the same basic faith.
Their very presence is an encouragement to each other.
Somebody might be there whom one might not associate
instinctively with church – but there he/she is and it gives others a
boost. When they sing together or recite the responses together
they are expressing their community of spirit. The common
recitation of the 'Our Father' deserves to be highlighted – this is
the prayer that Jesus gave us, the prayer that identifies Christians
of all denominations, that expresses all that needs to be said in
prayer. It is a profession of faith even more appropriate than the
Creed.

Many will remember seeing on television the funeral Mass of Pope
John Paul II, when heads of state took part in vast numbers. It
was a breath-taking moment when they turned to each other and
exchanged the sign of peace, putting aside even for the moment all
antipathies, all self-interests, all the injustices committed in their
names. While it might be argued that a handshake did not
necessarily mean anything further beyond the ceremony,
nevertheless even the gesture recognised that the only language

that made sense in that context was the language of peace. On what other occasion could such an exchange have taken place?

Even the simplest weekday Mass can be a beautiful and uplifting event. The preparation of the lectern (the 'altar of the Word'), of the altar, the lights, the spotless cloths, the vestments, the large impressive books, the procession to the sanctuary – all these details attended to with loving care create an atmosphere of something special about to happen, a piece of living theatre.

A brief but thoughtful explanation of the scripture readings, put in the context and against the background of the whole book, can bring an otherwise meaningless passage to life. (Weekday readings are referred to in the chapter on 'The Bible' as a possible structure for studying the Bible).

The actions of the Eucharist can be as impressive as the words: the focus on the bread and wine, the little bell calling our (perhaps wandering) attention to something great that is happening or about to happen, the priest's outstretched arms in prayer, supplication and greeting, embracing the whole congregation, the lifting up of the bread and wine, now the Body and Blood of Christ, the solemn words of consecration, the breaking of the bread in order to share it, Holy Communion.

In parenthesis, one might remark what a precious gift from God is the ability to sing. How it raises the spirits to sing even if nobody is listening! What simple and innocent entertainment it is when family and friends celebrate together and express their celebration in song! Singing together requires harmony, and expresses unity of spirit. When the Welsh people, in their inimitable way, sing their national anthem before a rugby match, together they express their pride in and devotion to their homeland.

It is such a pity that choral singing seems to be disappearing from many of our schools, especially secondary schools. It is also a pity that singing at football matches has taken on an aggressive tone, lampooning the other team – all good fun, no doubt, but making a mockery of the gift of song.

All the more reason then, why the music at Mass should be able to raise the heart and cheer the spirit. There is no excuse for poor music nowadays. Modern technology provides the means of having good music even in the smallest congregation, even where there is no musician willing and able to lead. Playing CDs or DVDs is no more artificial than using a microphone.

Worship

Religious ritual is essentially worship of God. It recognises that God is great, creative, powerful but also compassionate, merciful, our loving parent. We praise God, not because He demands it, much less because He needs it, but because we find Him praiseworthy.(1) When the sun shines on a spring day and the buds have burst into fresh green leaves, the spring flowers bringing colour and brightness to the scene, we say 'What a beautiful day!' We cannot keep it to ourselves, and want others to share our enjoyment.

When we praise God, we express an option for God and all that He signifies for us. It becomes an expression of commitment, of choosing His way when we return to our secular duties.

One of the prefaces for weekdays in the Mass says,

You have no need of our praise,
yet our desire to thank you is itself your gift.
Our prayer of thanksgiving adds nothing to your greatness,
but makes us grow in your grace.

To the Priest

Sunday Mass is a great opportunity for the priest. All these people have come voluntarily to listen to the Word of God, to hear it explained and applied to their lives, to engage in prayer and worship, led and assisted by the priest. Of all the good works that a priest may do, none touches the lives of so many people as the Mass he celebrates on Sunday. It deserves his very best effort and it is to him, in particular that the rest of this chapter is devoted.

The priest, especially a parish priest is beset on all sides with preoccupations: the governing body of the school, the parish hall and its social events, finances, preparation for the sacraments, all the various groups that are working in the parish; people call and need his advice and support, documents signed etc. Some priests enjoy the collaboration of a large and competent number of lay people. Even then, ultimate responsibility rests with him. It is not altogether surprising that sometimes he arrives at Saturday night, feeling jaded, almost taken by surprise that to-morrow is Sunday, desperately trying to put words together for the following day.

It would be easy to lecture such priests and tell them what they should do. The problem for them is not so much time, as a mind filled with preoccupations that make it difficult to focus attention on something as distant as the following Sunday, and to rise above them to things of the spirit.

Nevertheless, it is worth repeating that the Sunday Mass is the greatest opportunity imaginable to connect with the people who have come to Mass freely, the Mass which is described as the gathering of all our best efforts, hopes and aspirations and also the source of our inspirations and spiritual energies for the week ahead.

Pope Benedict XVI has written with great feeling about 'The Spirit of the Liturgy'(2), written when he was still Cardinal Ratzinger but only a couple of years before he was elected Pope. He is concerned at some of the ways in which he has observed the liturgy being celebrated. Priests can take liberties in the hope of engaging the people, especially the young. What the Pope emphasises is that especially the Eucharistic Prayer be focussed on God, and that we ought to ensure that the object of attention is not any individual (including the celebrant) or group which may be enacting some aspect of the liturgy (followed by a round of applause). He mentioned the appropriateness of all facing in the same direction for the Eucharistic Prayer including the celebrant, together intent on God, facing east where possible, the rising sun being the symbol of resurrection. This was interpreted as his desire to 'return to saying Mass with your back to the people'. He was so upset by this interpretation that he wanted to erase that detail from the second edition of his book and had to be persuaded to leave it intact. It is not the details that concern him but that the centre of attention be God.

The following are some suggestions, made with respect and great diffidence that might be helpful:

Preaching

Prepare, prepare, prepare: We need to find space, quiet, peace to reflect on the scripture readings for the following Sunday. The only time that the busy priest can be sure of peace and quiet is early morning. Allocate half an hour before breakfast from Tuesday onwards to read, study and reflect on the scripture each morning for the following Sunday.

Commentaries can help in enlightening us on aspects of the readings. Model homilies can also help. But the most valuable homily we can preach is when we are articulating what is important to us in our faith – it is surprising how difficult that can be. It will repay a priest for the rest of his ministerial life to apply his mind and identify what it is that keeps him going. Other sources can spark off an idea, a train of thought that sets us on our way.

Articulating our faith does not mean autobiography. Rather it enables us speak from the heart rather than repeat what we have read. The words and thoughts of others that we read might seem beautiful and impressive besides anything I could produce. But what matters is that my words, however poorly they may seem to me, is that they are <u>mine</u>, and come from the depths of my own faith. As one priest said, 'It may be only tuppence-ha'penny worth, but it is <u>my</u> tuppence-ha'penny worth.'

We should keep an eye out for events in the world that are of concern to people, such as the credit crunch, such as where was God during the tsunami? As the well-worn advice to preachers goes, 'Have the Bible in one hand and the newspaper in the other.' There may be something in the readings that would be relevant to such events.

Be positive. It is so easy to condemn sin, to say 'don't'. It is not necessary to moralise. What people need from us is uplift. The life of Jesus, his teaching, his interaction with people speaks for itself and is an endless source of inspiration. He was so gentle and understanding, so positive and encouraging, speaking harsh words only to those who laid heavy burdens on others. Preachers, beware!

'Tell us about God.' That was the response of a group of businessmen to clergy who asked them at a conference what they, the clergy, could best contribute to life in the inner city. Where else will people hear about God if not from the preacher or homilist? Words will always be inadequate, as we said in the chapter on God but the Gospel is our source, and our own faith the ground where the Gospel takes root for us.

Tell the truth. Of course, we tell the truth! How dare anybody suggest otherwise? But there are times when the truth about the Church or some of its representatives is embarrassing and hurtful. Even then, the truth must be spoken, not suppressed or obfuscated. The temptation is to talk about something else, persuading ourselves that the people might be scandalised if they knew the full story! As the Church has learned from bitter experience, the people will be much more scandalised by economy with the truth. If there is one organisation on the face of this earth that should never fear the truth, however painful, surely it is the Church of Christ.

Many priests agonise over their homilies. They feel inadequate, lacking the eloquence of which they are aware in others. Who knows what touches the hearts of our listeners? Sometimes a few awkward words, spoken from the heart, touch people in a way that a more entertaining homily may not. There may even be one person for whom a few words were what they needed to hear at that time. To be complimented on the homily is always encouraging, but does not necessarily mean that it has achieved its purpose. We do our best and leave the rest to the Holy Spirit.

The Whole Mass

While most priests prepare themselves for the homily, not so many prepare themselves for the Mass in general.

The Introduction: The format given in the Missal is: *As we prepare to celebrate these sacred mysteries, let us call to mind our sins.* To the writer, this seems a very cold and depressing introduction to the greatest celebration of our faith. Thankfully, the missal allows the celebrant to use his own words.

The introduction to the Mass can be important for the people. They come from a busy, hectic life, their minds full of all the things of the world. They need a little help to engage in the spirit of what they are about to celebrate, to 'lift up their hearts'. That help must come from the celebrant.

They might be reminded of God's benevolent presence among them, within them as they gather in His name; aware indeed of human frailty but in the context of God's strength, goodness and mercy; reminded that they are not alone, a tiny group in a remote place but that they are united with millions throughout the world who likewise gather on the Sunday to praise and worship the same Lord; they might even be encouraged by telling them what a great act of faith is all the effort they made to be present; one of the readings may have something inspiring and appropriate.

But in order to do so, the celebrant must himself be recollected, have given time to collecting his own thoughts and spirit, then rehearsing a few well-chosen words that will lift the people and engage their attention - and the words do need to be few and therefore, well chosen. He needs to ensure that the time before Mass is spent in quiet prayer and recollection.

It is also important that he develop respect for and empathy with the people before him, whom he is about to lead in worship. A priest writes of 'connecting' with the people – the invisible, intangible vibrations that nevertheless connect even 'across a crowded room'. They can come only from the heart. He must restrain the inclination we humans seem to have to find fault: restrain the irritation he may feel at some wandering in late, at an unruly or crying child, at one of his helpers who chooses to go walkabout during his homily while the eyes of all turn as one to watch this sideshow! The priest might refer back to what has already been said – the goodwill that has brought all these people here and, on the whole, their desire to be spiritually nourished.

The Eucharist: A priest might ask himself how often does he stop and meditate on the Eucharist, which he celebrates several times in the week. There is the real danger that he becomes so familiar with the words that they trip off his tongue without much reflection, even, God forbid, that he becomes bored by them.

It is suggested, then, that every Eucharist, especially on Sunday, is preceded by some meditation on the act of worship about to be performed, perhaps some part of it. The Preface, the 'holy, holy', the invocation of the Holy Spirit, the words of consecration, the mysteries of our faith, the doxology, the Our Father, Holy Communion: there is endless material for prayerful reflection.

....

All of this may be daunting to the priest, who even on Sunday morning is torn in different directions by all the details to be dealt with, including somebody asking for confession. The best prepared priest will experience distractions at Mass, even at the most solemn moments, as did so many of the saints. There is no formula, but a priest who is clear about the priorities will find a way. As with our homilies, we can but do our best.

There is no doubt that the priest's own fervour and faith, his love for the Mass he is celebrating communicates itself to the people in the congregation, young and old. Then there is no need for extraneous happenings to engage the interest of the people. Their wrapt attention is their response to 'the faith that is expressed in love' (3).

1. see CS Lewis *Reflections of the Psalms,* chapter on *A Word about Praising*
2. *'The Spirit of the Liturgy'* by Joseph Cardinal Ratzinger, publ. Ignatius Press 2000.
3. Galatians 5:6

7. THE BIBLE

Reference has been made several times to the Bible. In any effort to write about our Christian faith, it is inevitable that one would quote from, refer to, consult the Bible. It is the ultimate source of everything to do with our faith.

The purpose of a short chapter like this is to open up what, for many Catholics are closed books. For one making a decision to read and study the Bible, it is a daunting prospect. The Jerusalem Bible, with brief introductions and notes, has over 2,000 pages. The New Jerome Biblical Commentary before bibliography and index, has over 1,400 large pages of small print. Where does one begin?

It is only in relatively recent times that Catholics have been encouraged to read and study the Bible for themselves. Until then it was presumed that the Church would teach them what they needed to know and explain to them what it meant. Pope Pius X founded the Biblical Institute in Rome for the study of Scripture. The much-maligned Pope Pius XII made a break-through when he wrote an encyclical letter in 1943, *'Divino Afflante Spiritu'* encouraging bible study at all levels, and this encouragement was furthered by the Second Vatican Council in one of its constitutions *'Dei Verbum'*.

Study of the Bible

A popular and growing practice is what is called *lectio divina* or sacred reading, the Latin title coming from a long-standing monastic practice. A group of people meet regularly to reflect on a passage of scripture, reading, listening to each other's reflections, perhaps with some background from a competent scholar, and then, prayerful meditation.

This is different from Bible study, though they are more complementary than mutually exclusive. Bible study is a more academic approach, studying the background, the purpose, the style of a particular book which then enables us read it with greater understanding and appreciation.

A group that meets regularly for bible study is a great support for many, who would find the task of delving into the bible alone too daunting. Ideally the group would be led by somebody well versed in scripture. This is not always possible. The next best option is to form a small team of members willing to study together in succession the books of the bible, with the help of commentaries and to lead the group sessions. Everybody present at these sessions should have their bible with them so that they may discover where the book is, and get an idea of its shape, purpose and content.

Following the plan of the weekday Lectionary (the book of scripture readings for use at Mass) is one way for breaking into the Bible. We are given a structure such that over a two-year period, reading a little each weekday, one covers every book of the Bible, not the whole of every book, but sufficient to give an impression of each book.

Each year, the three synoptic Gospels are read continuously, beginning with Mark, then Matthew, then Luke, interrupted by Advent, Lent and Easter season, when appropriate passages are read, John's Gospel being read especially during the Easter season. The first reading each day is from the remaining books of the

Bible, both Old and New Testament. The first reading is always followed by a psalm, from the prayer and hymn book of the Jews.

A certain amount of investment is necessary. One needs a Bible, preferably one with adequate introductions to each of the books, and explanatory notes. One also needs a weekday missal. Even if it is not feasible to go to Mass each day, the missal contains the readings for each weekday, which is the structure already referred to. These books cost more than one might expect but then tend to last a lifetime.

Understanding the Stories

It is essential to have a commentary. The books of the Bible were written thousands of years ago. They were written in a style that is different from that to which we are accustomed. Story-telling is often their way of conveying a profound truth. Where we would use abstractions like 'good' and 'evil', 'right' and 'wrong', the Old Testament tends to write about good people and bad people, those who do right and those who do wrong. When they condemn the bad people and rejoice in how God has sorted them out, we tend to recoil, having in mind the delicate distinction between sin and sinner and the later example of Jesus in not condemning human weakness.

The historical accuracy of every detail of the story is less important than the overall message, less important to know what exactly happened, than to understand what it means. The message is always one of hope, that goodness would prevail and that wickedness would perish

The following quotation from *Dei Verbum* is relevant to understanding the Bible:

One *should carefully investigate what the sacred writer really intended ... and must have regard, among other things for 'literary forms'. For truth is proposed and expressed in a variety of ways, depending on whether a text is history of one kind or another, or whether its form is that of prophecy, poetry or some other type of speech. ... For the correct understanding of what the sacred writer wanted to assert, due attention must be paid to the customary and characteristic styles of perceiving, speaking and narrating which prevailed at the time of the sacred writer and to the customs men normally followed at that period in their everyday dealings with one another.* (n.12)

The births of various figures, Isaac, Samson, Samuel, John the Baptist, of Jesus himself were heralded by a visitation from a godly person, perhaps an angel, after which the mother became pregnant, to the amazement of everybody. In the case of Jesus, his birth was announced by an angel to the shepherds, angels sang in the sky, a star led three wise men from the east to where he was. In each case, the precise relation of facts, the wonderful and extraordinary events leading up to the birth, matter less than what they signal, namely that the child was destined by God for a special mission.

The Word of God

To convince a non-believer that the Bible is the Word of God, God's way of revealing Himself to the world, the authentic source for knowing God's will, that is perhaps the most difficult of all the challenges to an evangelist.

In the Old Testament the holy men are quite forthright in claiming to speak for God. In the New Testament the writers are more discreet but equally insistent that through them the invisible God is speaking. One might respond that writers making claims about their own inspirations and revelations are not the most convincing witnesses.

In this, as in many other matters of faith, a scientific proof is not possible because we are not dealing with a scientific problem. That does not mean that a claim cannot be verified. *'By their fruits you shall know them'* (1), was the advice Jesus would give in assessing those who claim to speak for God. The Bible has stood the test of time, of incessant scholarly scrutiny, of comparison with human sciences to verify factual and historical references, of hostile efforts to ridicule it.

There is no doubt that lots of difficulties remain, difficulties of interpretation, of understanding. But countless generations have found and continue to find endless inspiration from its pages and books. There is something solid about it, an honesty that does not flinch from facts that a less scrupulous writer wishing to make a case, might conveniently overlook.

Taking a leap of faith and accepting that the Bible is the Word of God – even if we are not altogether clear what precisely that means – then we find that it all hangs together. The whole untidy jumble from the early chapters of Genesis, through the turbulent history of the people chosen by God, their battles, their victories, their disasters, an adulterous King David being chosen as the forefather of the Messiah, the prayerful psalms that complain about God as often as they praise Him, and eventually the Gospels: it is all one glorious story of human beings shuffling through life and managing to leave a mark which, somehow, inspires future generations. Really, only God could have made sense of it all!

The Old Testament

'Old' and 'New' Testaments are the titles used by Christians. What we call 'Old Testament' is, omitting a few of the lesser books, the 'Hebrew Bible' for the Jews. It has already been said that the Bible is a closed book for many Catholics. That is particularly true of the Old Testament, even for many priests.

The title of 'old' might suggest something that has been left behind and can usefully be discarded. That understanding would be a great mistake. Christians are indebted to the Old Testament and have inherited so much from it such as: the images of God; the moral code expressed by the ten commandments, the fourth to the tenth of which describe basic human rights enshrined by the modern world in the Declaration of Human Rights; the psalms which articulate an earthy spirituality and which, in spite of the prayers and writings of so many great Christian mystics and saints, have never been replaced and still form the core of the daily prayer of the Church.

Above all, there is the sense of a consistent direction being followed, from the call of Abraham who would become the father of a great nation, to Moses being instructed to lead God's people out of Egypt to the promised land, to King David for whom a 'house' was promised, i.e. his descendants, from among whom the Messiah would come. God's plan is at work through what often seem the most unpromising of events, until it finds its fulfilment in Jesus Christ. St Jerome is often quoted as saying 'Ignorance of scripture is ignorance of Christ.' He might just as usefully said, 'Ignorance of the Old Testament is ignorance of Christ.'

Dei Verbum expresses it as follows:

These books (of the Old Testament) .. *give expression to a lively sense of God, contain a store of sublime teachings about God, sound wisdom about human life, and a wonderful treasury of prayers, and in them the mystery of our salvation is present in a hidden way.* (n.15)

As has been noted in various places throughout this book, the overall story that emerges from the Old Testament especially is a process of growth, human beings coming to terms with the world about them, trying to make sense of the ups and downs of life, trying to find answers to the profound questions that people ask, and continue to ask even today. For them, God is a living reality with whom they have a relationship, sometimes a stormy relationship on both sides.

Once it is accepted that the Old Testament describes a process of growth in understanding the world and the nature of God, it must not surprise us that some of the behaviour, even of the men of God, is not what we would want to imitate, in the light of what we learn later from the Gospel. Neither should particular prescriptions and prohibitions be taken as the final word on the subject but should be understood in the light of the Gospel.

It must be admitted that there are large sections of the Old Testament which are very tedious indeed, for example lengthy denunciations by the prophets of various leaders and tribes which can proceed for chapter after chapter. The prophets put into the mouth of God blood-curdling threats against the wicked, and then express great glee at the misfortunes that befall the wicked. Other books have long lists of members of the different tribes. It emphasises the need for commentaries and expert guidance in their study.

Another aspect of the Old Testament that can be off-putting is the violence perpetrated by God's people and often at the instigation of God's representative. (How Samuel 'cut to pieces Agag', to show Saul how God wanted him to deal with foreign princes, is probably the most horrible example, cf. 1 Samuel, 15:33.)

Our human understanding of God began with some very crude assumptions which, over the centuries were gradually refined. God's chosen people (the good) were in constant conflict with the gentiles (the bad). It took a revolutionary pronouncement by Jesus, 'Love (even) your enemies' to get to the heart of relationships between peoples and nations, recognising all people of all nations as our brothers and sisters, all equally children of the one God.

The appeal of the one, true God to all nations was foreseen and foretold by the prophet Isaiah, all people flocking to the mountain of the Lord, while the psalmist calls on all nations to praise the Lord. Both Isaiah and the psalmist, however, elsewhere denounce pagan nations and celebrate God's hand when raised against them. The nations flocking to the mountain of the Lord remained a dream.

Writers in the New Testament, especially the evangelist Matthew were at pains to point out how an event in the life or ministry of Jesus was foreshadowed in the Old Testament, and how the new is a continuation and fulfilment of, and not a rejection of the old.

The New Testament

The New Testament comprises the four Gospels, Acts of the Apostles, various apostolic letters, especially those of St Paul, and the Book of Revelations.

Most Christians will be familiar with the Gospels. They are, on the face of it simple books. They are not, however as simple as they might seem. They are not strictly biographies of Jesus. The synoptic Gospels (Matthew, Mark and Luke) have as their express purpose to convince their readers that Jesus was the Messiah. They go about this task in a very subtle way. They do not beat us about our heads with arguments and 'proofs'. Rather they hint. They describe the wonders, the healings, the power exerted over evil spirits and over the forces of nature, and always out of compassion for the sufferers. They quote texts from the Old Testament that are parallel to the events they are describing. They leave readers to draw their own conclusions.

John's Gospel, written much later and therefore presuming his readers were familiar with the synoptic Gospels, assumes from the first words that Jesus is the Son of God: *In the beginning was the Word .. the Word was God .. the Word was made flesh.* John describes a limited number of incidents in the life of Jesus, followed by a discourse spoken by Jesus to expound a deeper understanding of what has taken place.

Paul's letters are in response to queries he received from places where he had preached the Gospel. They are, therefore, personal, sometimes scattered and bitty, rather than an organised catechism. Paul expresses his faith in personal and passionate terms. He establishes a fundamental principle of the Gospel: that it is not a code of rules but a person, a warm, attractive human person, into whose very being Paul would be happy to be absorbed, the person of Christ. *'Let this mind be in you which was in Christ Jesus,'*(2) he said, and again, *'I live now, not I but Christ lives in me.'*(3)

The Acts of the Apostles describe life for the first Christians after Jesus had departed, the idealism of the early Christian communities. It tells of the coming of the Holy Spirit and how this transformed the apostolic community. Timid frightened men now went out fearlessly, and regardless of consequences, proclaimed to the world Jesus crucified and risen from the dead. Gradually and painfully, they made a breakthrough in moving outside their own Jewish community and preaching the Gospel to the pagans. Paul became the great apostle of the gentiles. The later chapters are devoted to the missionary journeys of St Paul along the coastline of Eastern Mediterranean, preaching at first to the local Jewish community and then to the Gentiles, the pagans.

The final book is the most difficult book of all to read, Revelations, based on visions of the writer, called John, though not necessarily the John of the fourth Gospel. Revelations repays reading, written as it was at a time of great difficulty for Christians in their faith, with its message of hope. It is a poetic story of the struggle between good and evil in the world, with the good ultimately prevailing.

....

The Bible is the Word of God for us. There we find all the sources for our religious faith. It tells the story of ordinary, weak, fallible human beings in their search for meaning and their awareness of God, until they find fulfilment in the Son of God made man, Jesus Christ, whose life and teachings are told in the Gospels.

1. Matthew 12:33
2. Philippians 2:5
3. Galatians 2:20

8. SEX and SEXUALITY

The writer thought long and hard before deciding to write this chapter. He is familiar with the usual objection, 'What can one dedicated to a life of celibacy know about sex?' Oh, yes? The writer suggests to those who think that way that they try celibacy for a couple of years. They will then discover a great deal about their sexuality, about the constraint that is not negative, but a positive channelling of one's affective energies in a direction other than towards an intimate relationship with another person. The priest, the religious directs his life towards ministry. That does not make him superior to, better than, more dedicated than anybody else, but it is his way.

Of course, celibacy goes against the accepted wisdom of the present age. It is not easy, but then the life of a devoted husband, wife, father, mother is not easy either. Both have their rewards. Celibacy can only be a positive influence in one's life by coming to terms with one's sexuality, by accepting the sexual urge as a constructive part of one's make-up and by channelling that power into a life of ministry. It takes a lifetime of effort to get the right balance but, on the way, one develops a greater understanding of and compassion for the human condition.

The other great objection in modern times arises from what have become known as 'the scandals', and they are scandals indeed, the all too numerous cases of priests and religious brothers sexually abusing children. The scandals were aggravated by the incompetent way some bishops and religious superiors handled them, at times sadly being 'economical with the truth', endeavouring to cover up, moving the offenders to another area, where unfortunately they continued their mischief. It is easy to criticise with hindsight, as it is true that, in the early stages of child abuse becoming widely known, not only bishops, but social workers and police were equally at a loss to know how best to proceed. What was not realised initially was the permanent damage done

to the victim, especially when the abuse was continuous over a long
period.

Priests and religious who have lived responsibly in their relationships
experience great anguish at the violation and corruption of children by
their colleagues, the very ones consecrated to recognising their dignity
and promoting their well-being. They feel the shame and disgrace which
is spewed indiscriminately by some over all priests and all religious.

In favour of the Church it must be said that, as with all scandals, they are
created by a small minority, though even one is too many. Critics of the
Church leaped at the opportunity. The result was much damage to the
credibility of the Catholic Church, especially in anything it might need to
say about sex.

Furthermore, the Church has endeavoured to come to grips with this
problem, establishing clear procedures for dealing with accusations (and
there have been false accusations too), ensuring that all cases are dealt
with fully and properly, involving the police where there is a case to be
answered.

In the longer term, there is something positive to emerge from what has
been a grim experience for the Church. There is a new spirit of humility
within. Humility must not be confused with fear or loss of confidence in
its mission. Humility is awareness of one's frailty, which induces
understanding of the frailty of others, an understanding of the burdens
they often bear and less inclination to dominate or to condemn.

In some countries, especially Ireland and the United States, the Catholic
Church has been rich and powerful. Large institutional buildings, often
surrounded by manicured lawns and colourful gardens, testified to a
body well endowed by its people. Many of these are no longer functional
because of the demise of the religious congregation that ran them, or

because they had to be sold to pay compensation to victims of sex abuse. The coffers of several dioceses and of some religious congregations have been well and truly emptied. Does not this state bring us closer to the Lord, who depended for his meals on the generosity of others and had not where to lay his head?

In these countries, some churchmen had a subtle but powerful influence politically. A word or a hint to a minister could ensure that the Church's interests, its institutions were protected. That power tends to corrupt applies to ecclesiastics as much as to anybody else. Such political influence is no more. The Church's influence now will depend on its 'authority from within' as previously described.

It can truthfully be said that as a result of the scandals, the Catholic Church in countries where it was once rich and powerful, has been brought to its knees – and that is no bad posture for it to take.

That its credibility in the eyes of the world has waned does not render invalid what it says. This chapter endeavours to show that all we understand by 'sex and sexuality' is something wonderful and something beautiful.

Sex

'I am firmly convinced,' said the young actress innocently to an interviewer in the late 1950s, 'that sex is here to stay.' The great and the learned tittered condescendingly, but everybody knew what she meant and everybody knew how right she was.

The word 'sex' has entered the modern vocabulary to mean what it means, where formerly it meant 'gender'. 'Sexuality' is a much broader term, referring to the whole person in relation to another or to others. It embraces emotions and feelings, affection and compassion.

There is no need to spell out how traditional taboos have gradually disappeared over the years, one by one. Much of this is thanks to what is known now as 'the entertainment industry', though whether they created or responded to a mood in society is open to debate. Television shows have become more and more explicit in their references to and portrayal of the sexual act, and other entertainment media have followed. There seems to be competition to see who can be the most daring. The problem is that once a particular line has been crossed, once a particular word has been used or a steamy scene shown, then it is no longer daring to cross that line again, so that the line of tolerance must be pushed farther and farther along.

Hence, the sexual interaction between two individuals is described in detail in much of modern literature, is portrayed almost without restraint on our screens, cinema and television, ever more daring, leaving little or nothing to the imagination.

At the same time that the portrayal of the sexual act becomes ever more explicit, so too the language associated with it becomes ever more explicit. The language however, tends to be not the biological terminology but the crude verbiage of the streets – words that parents would not allow their children to use, words that would not be spoken on a public occasion, but which now are common currency on some television and radio programmes, in pop songs. The extraordinary thing is that, to judge from their reactions, audiences who are supposed to be sexually liberated and to have a relaxed attitude to sexuality, still howl with laughter at references to genital organs or sexual interactivity.

Not everybody finds such references and what is called 'swearing' to be funny. It seems to be a short-cut that some comedians, lacking imagination and real humour, find it necessary to take, perhaps at the instigation of their directors. Many in the audience are still outraged and offended at the crude and brutal terminology often used. The BBC in early 2009 had to take drastic action in response to protests against two well-known comedians.

Relationships

Does it matter what sort of language is used? Yes, it does. Some words and language are crude and ugly and create a crude and ugly association. The words often used to describe the sexual act are often brutal, conveying dominance and power. If children, as they grow up learn only in the schoolyard or on the street about the procreation of babies, about sexual activity, in the vernacular that is current, this forms their attitudes. Sex becomes something forbidden but fun, frowned on by adults, enjoyed by youth. For some, it becomes something dirty and disgusting. Attitudes developed during their formative years are bound to affect their ability to establish satisfactory relationships in adult life.

Some years ago, a prominent Catholic writer, a married man, a consultant psychiatrist wrote:

> *The real evil of our age is not the permissiveness of sexual pleasure, but the impermanence of relationships whereby, through transience and divorce, human beings become stepping stones of temporary exploitation where the whole person is never engaged.* (1)

The key word is 'relationships'. There is probably no factor more important for human happiness in this world than the ability to establish and maintain healthy human relationships.

Unfortunately, it is emerging ever more clearly that the acceptance of teenagers becoming 'sexually active' at an ever diminishing age, is having disastrous consequences. What an innocent teenager does not and cannot understand is that an intimate sexual relationship causes an emotional explosion, that looks for affection at a depth which the partner, perhaps more experienced, may have no intention of returning.

This can lead either to grievous hurt which will colour the innocent's attitude to relationships in future, or to a hardening of heart and an attitude of 'if you cannot beat them, join them'. There is also an alarming increase in the prevalence of disease transmitted by sexual activity.

The Catholic Church insists that the intimacy of sexual intercourse is consistent only with commitment. The very nature of the act, physically and emotionally, expresses a giving of self that is total and that finds its full expression in marriage, where the partners commit themselves to each other 'till death do us part'. Casual sex without commitment is expressing something that is not meant to be taken seriously.

The stance of the Catholic Church is said to be 'unrealistic nowadays', that teenagers are going to indulge in sex anyhow and that the only realistic approach is to 'educate' them in the use of contraception and 'safe sex'. But reflecting on the consequences both short-term and long-term of casual sex, especially the effect on the ability to establish and maintain long-term relationships, one might well ask 'Who is it that is being unrealistic?'

Is there so little faith in younger people that adults in their wisdom have decided there is no point in appealing to their better nature, no point in presenting ideals of care and concern for other people, that the only thing that interests the young is self-indulgence and the present moment?

Education

Public authorities are realising the damage that is being done and are endeavouring to introduce into schools education in relationships under the broader heading of sex education. One hopes their efforts will be of assistance too to parents. One ventures to suggest that sex education and education in relationships cannot be put in a compartment, isolated from the education of the whole person, and all the qualities that go to make up one's personality.

There are basic human qualities which need to be taught to children, because they do not come easily or naturally: thoughtfulness for others, respect for others, sensitivity to their feelings, learning by doing, for example taking their share of household chores as a full member of the family community.

Modesty

Education in healthy human relationships cannot be reduced to simply saying 'Don't or else', spelling out the negative consequences. There is a word that expresses the positive, namely 'modesty', an old-fashioned word that deserves to be rescued from the cupboards, dusted down and rehabilitated.

It might be relevant to quote from a survey of teenage girls made in 2008 by teen magazines 'Bliss' and 'Women's Aid', quoted in the 'Guardian' (4 December 2008). The survey discovered that nearly a quarter of 14-year olds had been forced to have sex or to do something sexual they did not want to, and that over half of 14- and 15-year-olds had been humiliated in front of others by someone they were seeing.

These results suggest that modesty is still a reality for many even if the word is rarely used. Modesty is not the same as prudery. Prudery is based on disgust and fear. Modesty is based on reverence and respect. Modesty means dignity, based on respect for self and respect for the other person. It means understanding, valuing and being at peace with the functions of the body. It means appreciating how the genitals are the means of male and female cooperating with God in procreating a new human life, and reverencing the dignity of the act where this union takes place.

St Paul says, in his blunt way, *to fornicate is to sin against your own body,* and, in his inspiring way goes on, *Your body is the temple of the Holy Spirit, who is in you since you received him from God.* (1 Cor. 6:18,19)

Is it all bad, then?

Does this mean that the more relaxed attitudes to sex since the 1960s are all bad? By no means. It is no longer frowned upon to express affection in public, not only couples in love, but, for example, a father greeting his adult son with a kiss, friends greeting each other with a hug. It is less difficult to speak about one's feelings, one's affection. Parents and teachers are now encouraged to answer their children's questions truthfully, when they ask where babies come from, gradually informing them according to their desire to know, and their ability to understand.

With sex, extreme attitudes and behaviour attract attention. 'Celebrities' who are discovered to have casual sex with another 'celebrity' or with a prostitute will attract publicity, make the headlines, which has the effect of creating the impression that this is normal behaviour. On the other hand, a statement from one of the Catholic Church's congregations in Rome on anything remotely connected with sex will produce headlines, *'Vatican condemns ...'* Yet neither extreme portrayal represents normality nor the full truth, the ordinary spouse faithful to the end, the struggle many have to retain their ideals of sexuality with more ups than downs, the Vatican endeavouring to remind the world that there are higher values that contribute more to human well-being and happiness than short-term and instant self-indulgence.

Moderation has always been regarded as the ideal of virtue, *In medio stat virtus*, to quote the old Latin tag (except in love of God, say the theologians, and who could argue with that?). Yet we tend to publicise the extremes, which usually are the exception. The ordinary does not make news, nor does it attract attention. The faithful spouse does not make headlines. The couple who have weathered the ups and downs of rearing a family and have now reached contented retirement, appreciated by their children and cherished by their grandchildren, the headlines writers do not seek them out. They are, however, much nearer the norm than are the subjects of the lurid stories that figure so promptly in our popular news media.

1. 'Proposal for a New Sexual Ethic' Jack Dominian (Darton, Longman & Todd) p.60.

9. FREEDOM

He left home aged 16, insisting that he wanted his own space. He wanted to be free, free of parental supervision, free to invite whomsoever he wished to visit and to stay, freedom to come and go as he wished: in other words, freedom to do whatever he wanted. Ten years later, he returned home. He now wanted home just as it always was, the security, the warmth, the love that he would find only with his family.

It is a modern-day parable, reminiscent of the parable of the prodigal son in Luke's Gospel (1).

What Freedom is not

Freedom is not merely freedom *from* something. That sort of freedom is empty. Free from what, and then what? To wish to do only what one fancies is the way to an illusion. To do only what one fancies leaves one at the mercy of one's moods, tempers, lusts and passions. It becomes a form of slavery. One is no longer able to do what one ought because one does not feel like it.

Freedom is much more than absence of fear. Freedom is not supinely going along with the prevalent fashionable thought, so as not to be different. It is not servile obedience, for fear of incurring the wrath of another and perhaps punishment. It is not dishonesty, masquerading as defending a 'principle' which happens to promote one's comfort and advantage. It is not the cowardice that fears to take an unpopular stand in case it might attract ridicule of others whom we wish to cultivate.

Addiction to alcohol, tobacco or any of the other drugs now so easily available means being unable to face the day without a daily dose, or a dose several times in the day. Being driven by the pursuit of money or career, of prestige or power, of self-indulgence in food, drink or casual sex to the extent that it comes before all other considerations of family, friends, health of mind and body, means being at the mercy of a god that demands endless sacrifices.

A very successful businessman explained that the attraction of having lots of money was the freedom it gave him to do all sorts of interesting things. In the next breath he said that his diary was full for the following three years. Jokingly, he said that even his wife had to make an appointment to see him. What sort of freedom, one wondered, was that?

A rich young man approached Jesus wanting to know what he had to do to attain eternal life. (2) Diffident as always about laying burdens on people, Jesus reminded him of the ten commandments. The young man impatiently demanded more. Jesus gave him more. *'If you want to be perfect, go sell what you, give to the poor and come, follow me.'* He went away sad. That was more than he had bargained for. But the young man had rejected the possibility of being liberated from his money and possessions and of devoting his life to the pursuit of the divine.

What is Freedom?

To be free from outer constraint is the first basis for freedom. The punishment for crime is imprisonment, that is, being deprived of physical freedom to come and go as one decides. That is a very severe punishment. Those who complain of 'soft' regimes in prisons might reflect that to deprive people of freedom and subject them to the regime of prison, does not imply a need to further degrade and humiliate them. There is no need for outrage if prisoners are given turkey and plum pudding for their Christmas dinner. Those who are indignant at such 'molly-coddling' might ask themselves which they would prefer: turkey and plum pudding in prison or beans on toast at home.

Loss of freedom was experienced in its extreme by the hostages of the late 1980s in Beirut. They were subjected to the most humiliating and brutal treatment, always blind-folded in the presence of their guards. One of them, Brian Keenan tells how he and his cell-mate, John McCarthy used to have long philosophical debates against the background of their appalling conditions and experiences. They concluded: *Our world was not the monochrome morality, which defined and limited theirs* (their guards). *Even in these most deprived conditions we found within ourselves and within those shared discussions a more valuable and richer world than we had conceived of before. We were beginning to learn our freedom, the way Rousseau spoke of it. Captivity had re-created freedom for us. Not a freedom outside us to be hungered after, but another kind of freedom which we found to our surprise and relish within ourselves.* (3)

Freedom then seems to reside in the interior self.

'Blessed are the Meek'

In the sermon on the mount, Jesus begins with the beatitudes, one of which states *'Blessed are the meek'* (Matt.5: 5). It is also translated as 'Blessed are the gentle.' Meekness, gentleness might sound like softness, 'meekly' submitting to any pressure from without, 'gently' not wanting to offend by taking a strong stand on anything.

In fact, the original word, scholars tell us, means 'being in control of oneself'. Being at the mercy of one's moods, tempers, lusts and passions has been described as a form of slavery. Being in control of these emotions and urges is strength, the strength of being able to do what one ought and which, deep down, one wants to do. It is the strength of real freedom. Keenan tells how he and McCarthy maintained their dignity and their inner resolve, while some of their guards who inflicted beatings and humiliations upon them lived in fear of their chiefs.

Meekness knows how to deal with anger, a destructive force when unleashed. Anger is also destructive when allowed to bubble inside but unable to express itself. A calm sense of proportion, refusal to respond to injured pride, indifference to scoring points, an ability not to be too concerned about appearance or what others might think, shows control and strength. There is a time and a place to show anger, as Jesus did. Sometimes it is the only way that others, especially children get the message. He also said *'Blessed are those who hunger and thirst for justice'* (Matt.5:6). Sometimes a display of anger is necessary in the interests of truth and justice. But it is anger that has purpose, as distinct from an uncontrolled fit of temper, a directed as distinct from an undirected missile.

Discipline and Freedom

For many the two words 'discipline' and 'freedom' are contradictory. True enough, for many discipline is understood as something imposed from without, as it often is. It can be restricting and oppressive.

Yet we cannot live together in harmony without some restrictions imposed from without, for example, that cars drive on the left (or right in many countries) side of the road, and that they observe certain speed limits. Such restrictions recognise that whatever we do, we must recognise the rights of other people to go about their lives in peace and safety.

Laws for the common good can be accepted grudgingly, to be ignored whenever outside the watchful eye of the law enforcers, loopholes to be found wherever possible.   Or they can be seen as good sense in a civilised society and accepted internally as well as observed externally, because of a genuine concern for the well-being and comfort of others.

It surely is clear which mentality is that of the slave and which that of the free. St Augustine, in his Rule for his religious communities, concludes by encouraging his followers to observe all that is written *cum dilectione,* broadly translated as 'with cheerful love', *living not like slaves under a yoke, but like people living in freedom under grace.*(4)

'Love your neighbour as yourself.'

St Paul wrote with great feeling about the difference between mere external observance of laws and responding positively to laws by absorbing the spirit that led to their promulgation. He said that to *love your neighbour as yourself* summed up all the laws. Such love describes not an attribute but the whole person, a person liberated from self-absorption, a person able to transcend at all times mere self-interest and look to the common good, the well-being of the person next door.

Love your neighbour as yourself is surely the ultimate charter of freedom.

1. Luke 15:11-32
2. Matt. 19:16-22, Mark 10:19-22, Luke 18:18-23
3. Brian Keenan, 'An Evil Cradling', p.230 publ. Ted Smart, 1993
4. Rule of St. Augustine c.8

10. DIFFICULT QUESTIONS

In writing this book I wanted to confront some of the difficult questions that can cause a lot of anguish to conscientious people within the Church, anger among some who no longer want to belong, criticism from without.

Often there is misunderstanding, but not always. There are difficult questions to which there are no simple answers. I make no claim to provide a simple or even a satisfactory answer to any of the questions raised.

What I hope is that conscientious people who may feel torn between seemingly conflicting goods, will find re-assurance. Before God, you cannot be in a situation where, whatever you decide will be wrong. Nobody lives in an ideal world and sometimes it seems that the path of perfection is closed to us. Decisions made in conscience, formed especially by concern for the well-being of those about us cannot be wrong.

God who understands our difficulties and our frailty, also understands our goodwill.

CONTRACEPTION

The writer was returning from a holiday, passing through London one evening in late July 1968, to be confronted with newspaper billboards announcing that Pope Paul VI had just published an encyclical letter banning the use of the contraceptive pill and artificial contraception generally. Many of the same generation will remember exactly where they were when that news broke for them. The encyclical was entitled 'Humanae Vitae'.

That night on television a special edition of 'Panorama' screened interviews with a number of prominent Catholics who would normally have defended the Church. To-night was different. They were angry, bitterly angry with the Church they clearly loved. A long period of uncertainty had led many to make their own decisions. The Pope engaged in a period of consultation, the result of which was that he ignored the advice of his special commission and pronounced as he did.

The anger expressed that night was widespread. The encyclical was a watershed in the modern history of the Church. It is said that Pope Paul was so stricken by the hostile reaction that he never wrote another encyclical. For some, it was the last straw and they abandoned the Church. Others decided to make up their own minds regardless of the encyclical. Others still, took the message of the encyclical to heart and endeavoured to live by it.

The word 'conscience' was often heard. Conscience had to be the final arbiter. Some senior ecclesiastics took fright at such independence of thought and talked of the 'formed conscience', the conscience that could only be honestly formed by following the teaching of the Church.

It was the late 1960s. Rebellion against authority was in the air. Satire programmes on television lampooned sacred institutions in a way that would previously have been unthinkable. Unspeakable comment was made, unmentionable words used. Barriers tumbled and nothing could ever be the same again.

Now

New generations have grown up in an atmosphere of making up one's own mind – listening to others, but finally deciding for oneself. The new independence of spirit has led to a greater sense of one's worth and dignity; it has also led to life decisions being made on the basis of emotional likes and dislikes, rather than on the basis of traditional wisdom gleaned through centuries and millennia of life's experience.

We are told – it is not always clear on what basis, probably observing the size of families – that Catholics nowadays on the whole ignore what the encyclical *Humanae Vitae* prescribed.

Such has been the anger generated by the encyclical that discussion of marriage, of sex in a Catholic setting has become almost impossible, either in discussion groups or from the pulpit. Furthermore, any reference by the Church to an issue associated with, however vaguely contraception, is met with angry retorts if not derision. It also led to a loss of confidence among many priests, who feel at a loss in any discussion of the issues. They feel torn between their duty to defend the Church's teaching and the sympathy they feel in their hearts for good people they know, who cannot cope with the Church's prohibition in their circumstances. A tiny survey revealed that many young priests of the 21st century had never heard of *Humanae Vitae*, <u>never heard of it!!</u> This seems to suggest that drawing a veil over the issue is the way it is being dealt with even in some seminaries. If that is so, it seems a very unsatisfactory way to deal with anything.

The Positive

That the local Church and, in particular its preachers feel restricted in speaking about family and married life is a great loss to everybody, Catholic or not. Whatever about contraception, the issues of marriage and family are crucial for the well-being of society, and the Catholic Church takes a firm stand in support of both. It has something to say that the world needs to hear. Rather than get immersed in the details, it might be more profitable to endeavour to see behind the thinking on which the encyclical is based, to uncover the bigger idea.

The basis is an exalted, perhaps romantic notion of marriage, married love, the procreation of human life as an act of collaboration with God. Sexual intercourse is an act of total love, giving of self not only physically but totally, the natural outcome of which is the generation of a new human being. Parents will surely agree that within the context of the family, the birth of a child is an indescribable joy.

The love, the self-giving, the emergence of human life, the gradual growth of the child in the womb, the birth are human experiences of the highest order, to be cherished and to be protected against whatever might diminish them. Of course, there is pain – there is sacrifice in love and self-giving, there is pain in carrying an ever-increasing infant within oneself and then giving birth. Sometimes there is misgiving at the idea of supporting another child, especially if it was unexpected. While there are cases, too many cases, of children being unwanted and children being abused, on the whole children are cherished by their parents. When a teenage child complained there were too many in the family and not enough money to have things that others had, the father, having assembled the rest of the family asked, 'Which of them would you do without?'

Church statements speak of the family as an image of Christ and the Church. Families might feel that, however beautiful, this is not a faithful image of their family, where children quarrel, mother gets cross, father complains about money. This is the reality of human relationships and of running a household, they would say.

But sometimes our closeness to something in which we are emotionally involved makes us aware of the imperfections, the shortcomings, not adverting to the beauty and greatness that is the basic reality. The virtue of the family is that children can grow up through the various stages of infancy, childhood, adolescence, adulthood in an atmosphere where they are accepted as they are. As they grow up, more and more they assert individuality and independence, stretching the boundaries. Parents still love them even when exasperated by their increasing questioning of parental decisions.

The fact that the tensions of human relationships and of growing children can take place in an atmosphere where all concerned know they are still valued in spite of the occasional argy-bargy: that is love. The fact that parents constantly give of themselves and what they have and seek only the well-being of their children: that is love. The Gospel parable of the prodigal son who squandered his inheritance, was reduced to destitution, decided to return home in the hope of being accepted as a servant, and being effusively welcomed by the parent as a long-lost son, that parable will resonate in the hearts of many parents.

Some Consequences of Contraception

Returning to the encyclical: whether such an exalted understanding of marriage and the family justified the total ban on *'any action which ... is specifically intended to prevent procreation'* (1), is for the learned to decide, and for the rest to act according to what they believe is right for their marriage and relationship. The basic drive of the argument is respect of the spouses for one another, thoughtfulness for one another's condition and needs, and reverence for the source of human life.

It might be interesting to recall what the Pope saw as possible consequences of the use of contraception.

'How easily this course of action can lead to .. marital infidelity, and a general lowering of moral standards.'
'All people – and especially the young ... – need incentives to keep the moral law, and it is an evil thing to make it easy for them to break that law.'
'A man who grows accustomed to the use of contraceptive methods may forget the reverence due to a woman ... and reduce her to being a mere instrument for the satisfaction of his own desires.'
'Finally, ... who will prevent public authorities from favouring those contraceptive methods which they consider most effective?   .. they may even impose their use on everyone.' (2)

While there is no turning back of the clock, no way of un-inventing what is now commonplace, might not Paul VI have had a point in his observations that indicate where he was coming from?

However, one instinctively feels that the absolute condemnation of contraceptive methods within marriage (and the encyclical deals only with within marriage) is an intrusion too far into the intimacy of people's relationships. In the Gospel, Jesus when asked questions of detail, refused to become entangled but referred to the general basis for all that he was teaching, leaving it to individuals to apply the overall principles to the details of their private lives.

If it is the case that many Catholics, otherwise committed and observant, make their own decision about the use of contraception, then this is an indication of the truth seeping up from below rather than being imposed from above. The Second Vatican Council's document on 'The Church', speaking of the 'People of God' states

'The body of the faithful as a whole, anointed as they are by the Holy One cannot err in matters of belief. Thanks to a supernatural sense of the faith which characterises the People as a whole, it manifests this unerring quality when "from the bishops down to the last member of the laity", it shows universal agreement in matters of faith and morals.' (3)
(A footnote states that this was a favourite theme of Cardinal Newman.)

It would be an overstatement, however, to suggest that this quotation is a conclusive argument for a liberal understanding of *Humanae Vitae*. It does indicate, however, that an instinctive and conscientious response of people of genuine faith deserves to be heard. It makes a point that is not often aired in the Church and that deserves much reflection.

What the Encyclical does NOT say

Humanae Vitae is the final word of the Catholic Church on the use of contraceptives within marriage. Although often referred to, nothing has been added to it since 1968.

A burning question is when, in a marriage, one partner is infected with HIV, whether it is lawful to use condoms in that case. (It is surprising that commentators tell us that nobody takes any notice of the encyclical nowadays, and then blame the Catholic Church when condoms are not used in marriage to prevent transmission of disease.)

Paragraph 14 of the encyclical insists that *'sexual intercourse which is deliberately contraceptive'* is wrong, i.e. it is the <u>contraceptive intention</u> that the encyclical states is unacceptable. Paragraph 15 however states *'the Church in no way regards as unlawful therapeutic means considered necessary to cure organic diseases, even though they have a contraceptive effect.'*

Putting the two paragraphs together, it is fair to conclude that when the intention in using condoms is to prevent transmission of disease, even if the effect is contraceptive, it is not against either the letter or the spirit of the encyclical.

If this interpretation is correct, it needs to be said out loud. Many local clerics fear that any suggestion on their part of anything less than wholesale condemnation of any form of contraceptive for whatever purpose, under any circumstances, will bring swift retribution from the Vatican. Their fear might even be justified! Perhaps all, high and low, should read *Humanae Vitae*, especially paragraphs 14 and 15.

IN VITRO FERTILISATION

Bio-technology is proceeding at such a breath-taking rate that ethics is struggling to keep pace with it.

Ethics

Ethics is not the property of the churches. Ethics is the concern of every human being. Ethics enable us understand what it is to be human, what is in keeping with our human nature and our human aspirations. It also warns us of what might be damaging to our humanity, perhaps in the longer term of some procedure that appears attractive, sensible and compassionate here and now.

In the continuing debate that goes on every time bio-technology is topical, a correspondent wrote: 'Religion without ethics gives you al-Qa'ida; politics without ethics give you Auschwitz.' He might well have added: 'Medicine without ethics gives you Mengele-type eugenics.'

A concern for Catholic couples that seems to be increasing in frequency is the ethical nature of In Vitro Fertilization (IVF). It is well known that the Catholic Church does not approve. It is not a simple condemnation. The Church set out its reasons in a substantial document in 1987 (4), which has been reiterated but not changed on occasions since then.

Status of Human Embryo

The most basic issue is the status of the human embryo. The Church is not alone in regarding it as entitled to respect as for any human life from the first moment of conception (see previous chapter on 'The Church'). One of the problems with IVF is that the extraction of ova from the woman is quite a distressing procedure, the success rate is low and consequently several ova are extracted in one procedure. This is a problem that might be alleviated or even disappear with further advances in techniques. Meanwhile, assuming success is achieved, the question arises what to do with the remaining embryos. Can they be used for experimentation in order to seek cures for various illnesses? If not, how does one dispose of them? It is then a real matter of conscience.

The Unitive Element

The other issue is the opposite of the Church's stand on contraception. *'Any use of marriage must retain its natural potential to procreate human life. This doctrine is based on the inseparable connection ... between the unitive significance and the procreative significance which are both inherent to the marriage act.'* (*Humanae Vitae* n.12). Whereas the procreative element is lacking in the case of contraception, it is the unitive element that is lacking in the case of IVF, i.e. conception arising from the loving union of husband and wife.

This reasoning is based on 'natural law', rather than on any biblical teaching. Discussion of natural law is deep water indeed, beyond the scope of this essay. One might venture to suggest that a natural law in any particular case, i.e. the very nature of the things or actions in question, would be obvious to everybody. How obvious it is that the distinctive elements, 'unitive and procreative' are 'inherent to the marriage act' is debatable.

Nobody would argue that the perfect origin of human life is sexual intercourse between a married couple that leads to conception. The problem arises when this is not possible and science offers other possibilities. The Church does encourage the efforts of science to find a remedy for infertility, but always protective of human life and of spouses being cooperators with God in giving life to a new person.

There may be some consolation for Catholics who have resorted successfully to IVF, but feel worried about their stance with the Church in the following quotations from the Church's statement: IVF where there is no donor other than husband and wife *'is not marked by all that ethical negativity found in extra-conjugal procreation'* (n.5).

'Although the manner in which human conception is achieved with IVF cannot be approved, every child which comes into the world must in any case be accepted as a living gift of the divine Goodness and must be brought up with love.' (n.5)

HOMOSEXUALITY

One of the most vexed questions for the Catholic Church is its attitude to homosexuality. Not only is great hurt caused by the statement *'homosexual orientation must be seen as an objective disorder'*, but the scientific basis for such a statement is questioned.

In November 2005, a Vatican congregation excluded from admission to seminaries those with 'deep-seated homosexual tendencies' (5), an expression that was not explained and which is liable to cause great anxiety among some conscientious and good-living priests while discouraging some who may be thinking of the priesthood or religious life, and are aware of an inner conflict. Who is not aware of inner turbulence in regard to their sexuality, whether homosexual or heterosexual, whether within or without marriage, celibate or otherwise? But conscientious men might interpret this confusing phrase as excluding them from priesthood.

A crucial question is whether sexual orientation is of nature or of nurture. Is it inherent in some individuals or is it an inclination that develops depending on the circumstances and experiences of the individual's upbringing? Much study of the subject has been taking place and some results describe significant discrepancies in parts of the brain between homosexual and heterosexual men.

Civil Unions

In what is generally referred to as 'the developed world', attitudes changed greatly towards homosexuality in the second half of the twentieth century and since then. No longer are homosexual acts between consenting adults illegal, carrying a possible prison sentence as they once did. More recently, English law and others recognised what it described as a 'Civil Union', a union between people of the same sex, giving legal rights of inheritance, for example, to members of such a union. These developments reflect a more tolerant attitude of the public at large.

The positive aspect of the Catholic Church's attitude is its concern for marriage vows and the married life. Marriage is understood as between man and woman. From the beginning marriage has been and is to ensure the continuance of society, being the means of procreating children and providing them with the security and loving environment in which they can grow up. Family life of father, mother, children is for their personal happiness and well-being, but also ensures the future of the human race. The Church is emphatic that the family is the bedrock of society, and that the health of the society depends on the health of family life.

The Catholic Church is one body that makes an uncompromising stand on the sacred nature of married life, as defined, and on the sanctity of the marriage vows. Father, mother, committed to each other 'till death do us part', and children is the ideal and the norm. However, people can find themselves inextricably in circumstances which would not be regarded as ideal, but which cannot be changed without grave hurt to others. Such people deserve understanding and respect. It is surely basic humanity to ensure that a loving and lifetime union of two people should be accorded security, respect and dignity, whether or not one approves of their union.

Family of man, woman, children

It is unfortunate, however that many have chosen to describe the civil unions now allowed by the state as 'single-sex marriages', thus creating a confusion which is unnecessarily confrontational. Marriage of man and woman, and the bearing of children is the norm. That does not mean that marriage is threatened by exceptions. Some marriages do not bear children. Those who embrace priesthood or religious life live a life of celibacy, as do many lay people. Sometimes siblings continue to live together in the family home after the parents have died. They too need the protection of the law to give them the security of inheritance when one of them dies. None of these states would be seen as threatening married life in any way.

There is no doubt that the traditional family is under pressure by many of the values current in our world, especially the cry for individual rights without recognising individual responsibilities, and not always respecting the rights of others. Defending the family, however is not best done by condemning all other forms of human unions. It has already been suggested that the word 'condemn' is not part of the Gospel vocabulary. It was never Jesus' way to condemn those who are different, in order to bolster the good.

'Do not be afraid'

Jesus was continually reassuring his disciples, telling them 'Do not be afraid'. His Gospel is sufficiently robust to withstand all that can be thrown at it. There is the history of two thousand years and more in proof. It is robust because what it says is true and people through the centuries recognise its truth. The same can be said of the institution of marriage.

The spirit of the Gospel is so positive, so life-giving, so uplifting, so encouraging to weak human beings, and yet so strong, so firm, so uncompromising. It is indeed good news to the poor, the sick, the blind, the lame, the oppressed, as it is to the well-off, the healthy, the sighted, the nimble, the free. Why not also to those with 'deep-seated homosexual tendencies'?

VOCATIONS TO PRIESTHOOD AND RELIGIOUS LIFE

In the middle of the twentieth century, there was a surge of vocations to priesthood and religious life. As the gentry became impoverished and sold up their large houses and grounds, religious orders moved in, attaching large extensions to the original gracious residences to accommodate their aspirants and students. It was a fruitful period for overseas missions, the priests, brothers and sisters bringing education and health care to remote parts of the world, as well as the liberating message of the Gospel.

All that has changed. It might be remarked that the superabundance of consecrated people in that period was the exception in history and it is not surprising that it has not lasted. However, in the 'developed world', as we like to call ourselves, the pendulum has swung to the other extreme. The early twenty-first century is a time for deep reflection on the future of priesthood and of consecrated life in the Church.

Change was influenced by growing affluence and the wide spread of options for young school leavers. Lay groups now work overseas in a pastoral capacity, of famine relief, of providing medical care and education. The modern state provides free education and, in most developed countries free medical care. The contribution made in the past by many religious congregations and the opportunities for service that they offered are now available through other and secular means. While this development creates difficulties for a religious congregation, it is a development in which to rejoice.

There is also the question of celibacy which looms large and which is given a bad press. As a requirement especially for priesthood, its most vocal defenders tend to be official voices who often speak in a language that is difficult to follow. The modern culture that places such a heavy emphasis on sex as an essential element in life, that believes happiness is inconceivable without it, does not help.

There will always be a need for consecrated groups of people. There will always be, as suggested elsewhere (6) inspired individuals who have the vision to see what is needed at a particular time, and have the strength to pursue that vision, overcoming all the inevitable obstacles on the way.

What then?

What then? Married priests? Women priests? Why not, but if so it would require a change in mind-set. If priests are to be allowed to marry, it ought to be because the experience of marriage and family is seen as a valuable contribution to priesthood, and not simply to make up numbers. The same could be said of women priests, that their femininity and possible experience of married life and of motherhood are seen as factors that would enrich their priesthood, and, as for men, not simply to make up the numbers. Permanent deacons, where they are allowed to operate outside the sacristy, have shown what a good married man can contribute to the life of a parish. Other Christian churches have shown how effective married men and women ministers can be.

A necessary word

Arguments could rage forever about these issues. One might suggest that the real concern for attracting candidates to priesthood and religious life is at a deeper level. It might be described in one word: holiness.

Pessimists in the Church blame the Vatican Council of the early 1960s and the more humane theology that it expounded for many of the ills of the Church at present. Perhaps they might consider what other factors have influenced that of which they disapprove. It may or may not be a coincidence that the Vatican Council coincided with the revolution in mind-set and attitudes of the 1960s and 70s. Religious communities were not immune to the spirit of the age. Old disciplines were relaxed, authority questioned, individualism acquired a louder voice than the common good. One dares to suggest that the influence of the world of the 1960s and 70s was a more powerful force in changing religious life than was the theology of the Vatican Council. Change was indeed needed but the baby and bath-water metaphor applies. It became ever easier to insinuate a cosier way of life into religious communities, to emphasise the well-being, if not the comfort of the individual as more important than the community, where the 'cell' became so comfortable and so self-sufficient that it was scarcely necessary ever to leave it for traditional community practices, even for prayer. The criterion became being 'sensible', being 'realistic'.

Collaboration with Laity, and with other priests

There is much talk in priestly circles of 'collaboration with the laity', and with no small results to show. It could even be that the present and ever-looming 'shortage' of priests is a challenge to the lay members of the Church, to which many are responding. The Holy Spirit is guiding the Church into its future shape. It is noteworthy the numbers who are studying theology at tertiary level. Some train as catechists, leading parish groups preparing for sacraments, or adults about to be received into the Church, some direct the music ministry, some organise the parish liturgies, some even manage the parish finances! Much, if not all depends on the *beneplacitum* of the parish priest.

Collaboration with the laity is not the simple solution that is sometimes suggested. Lay groups can lead to little empire-building, there can be petty quarrels, closed minds, much talk and little action. A priest can be driven to distraction. The overall picture however, is that greater good is achieved by lay ministry than frustration caused. In any case, priests themselves are not immune to human frailty. Nothing is ever simple!

There is also a need to reflect on 'collaboration with other priests'. It is extremely difficult to get a group of priests to sit down together and to work out a cohesive plan to which all will contribute. There is such an emphasis on the power of the individual, 'my parish', 'nobody will tell me what to do in my parish', that it is extremely difficult to plan against the larger background of the diocese, of the church, of the people at large.

Holiness

To return to that word 'holiness': Holiness is not a grim rigidity, an obsession with rules, a determination to be miserable, an off-putting aloofness. It is quite the opposite. It is described as 'wholeness', being fully human, full of humanity. There is no better role model than Jesus, the Jesus of the Gospels. A heart for people, simplicity of life-style, strong in standing for the truth, gentle with the weak, unhurried with space always for prayer, never self-seeking, never using people – these are some of the characteristics which, however imperfect the individual may be, should identify the priest and the religious. These are the factors that are more likely to attract new members than all the promotional literature, CDs, websites etc., etc.

SUFFERING

Just as we were settling down after Christmas Day 2005, to relax in the peaceful aftermath of the hectic activities leading up to Christmas, we learned a word that was new to most of us but which since then has become seared into our vocabulary: tsunami.

This undersea upheaval caused a wave of prodigious magnitude followed by an ebbing that seemed to suck all the water out of the ocean. The scale of the devastation was unimaginable. Over 150,000 people died, countless numbers lost parents, child, beloved family, had their homes destroyed, their means of livelihood ruined, the local infrastructure uprooted.

Television, often with the aid of tourist amateur photography, brought us graphic images of individual suffering that were more powerful than all the statistics. Immediately there was an unprecedented world response to provide whatever was needed.

Why?

At the same time, the question was being asked, 'Why?' 'Why does a good and loving God allow these natural disasters? We can understand when innocent people suffer because of human wickedness, but not how God's created world can be so cruel.'

That is a question that has been asked from the time that human beings began to think and to rationalise about the world. In the Bible, the book of Job endeavours to deal with it – not very satisfactorily, as Job was compensated for his faithful acceptance of his condition, everything was restored to him and he lived happily ever afterwards. That is not everybody's experience.

However, he does establish that, in spite of his ordeals he is an innocent man, contrary to the popular belief articulated by his three 'comforters' that he must have done something terrible to have drawn upon himself such suffering. Jesus would later emphasise similarly, when asked who had sinned, was it the man born blind or his parents. Jesus replied that it was neither this man nor his parents who had sinned (John 9:3).

There is still no satisfactory answer to the 'Why?' even in our sophisticated world of the 21st century.

Where was God?

The other apparently similar but quite different question is 'Where was God?' during the tsunami. That is a question to which one can attempt an answer.

There is a story from one of the concentration camps during the 1939-45 world war, when a young man was being publicly hanged and all the inmates were paraded to watch. As the young man's body hung there, the teller was angrily asked by the man beside him, 'Now, where is your God?' He replied by pointing at the body. 'There He is', he said. (7)

God is not an abstraction, out there somewhere, in distant, isolated splendour. Our Christian faith is of God who came among us as one of us and shared our condition through to humiliation and death on the cross. He identified with the most despised and needy, *'As often as you did it (not) to one of these, my least ones, you did it (not) to me.'* (Matt.25: 40,45) He was able to identify with them because he himself had suffered. He experienced fatigue, homelessness, misunderstanding even from those close to him, hostility and, in the end, he, an innocent man was condemned in disgrace, forced to carry through the crowded streets the cross of the criminal on which he would die and then died in agony, experiencing something very close to despair.

Because he suffered, he has given dignity to all human suffering, the innocent who are condemned, imprisoned, tortured, those who bear heavy burdens in life, those who suffer excruciating pain, those who are disgraced publicly and their grieving family, those who fall and fail again and again and again, those who are tempted to lose hope.

The cross, once a sign of shame, is the great Christian symbol, a symbol of hope, of new life brought through suffering.

We find Jesus, Son of God, in those who suffer, physically or mentally. Since his ministry was healing and his preaching was love, we find him also in whoever supports and ministers to those who suffer. The good Samaritan is the archetype of those who pour healing oils on wounded souls. Jesus himself is our wounded healer.

Where was God, then in the tsunami disaster?

He was with each victim, drowned or crushed to death. He was with each survivor whose life, home, family, way of life had been torn apart. He was with each helper, government, organisation, individual who sought to enable afflicted people survive in the aftermath, and then begin to re-build their lives. He was with each one who contributed to the appeals, the governments with their millions, corporations with tens of thousands, individuals with hundreds or tens or singles or just the widow's mite. In all of this, He does not distinguish between religious affiliations.

Just as Jesus sought out the poor, the lame, the sick, the blind, the deaf and ministered to them with his healing power, so his Spirit is at the heart of all suffering people and of those who minister to them.

Response to Suffering

There is no way one can rationalise or explain away a tortured or dead child, a parent of young children stricken with terminal illness, a vigorous and healthy young man paralysed following a car accident, a couple traumatised as they survey their ruined home and livelihood. There is no way one can rationalise or explain away the sadistic power that degrades, humiliates and inflicts pain on helpless prisoners or on powerless children Such pain is an inescapable fact of human existence. It is a reality that we human beings not only have to live with but have to deal with, whether we understand it or not.

Suffering of others makes us pause and look at our own life, reminded that 'there but for the grace of God, go I' and that to-morrow it could be me. It helps us be thankful for what we have got, rather than discontented for what we have not. It arouses our compassion and draws out our better instinct to do what we can to help another.

In the aftermath of the tsunami, Kofi Annan, then secretary-general of the United Nations said, '*The past 11 days have been among the darkest in our lifetime. But they have also allowed us to see a new kind of light. We have seen an opportunity to heal old wounds and a long-running conflict. We have seen everyone pull together.'*

In the rescue and aid effort, there was a large military presence, battleships, helicopters, planes, personnel, all designed and trained to inflict damage and death, but now bringing life-giving sustenance and relief. One could not but think of the passage from the prophet Isaiah (2:4): '*They shall beat their swords into ploughshares and their spears into pruning hooks,'* even if only for a while.

All contributions and efforts from the least to the greatest had this in common: there was no self-interest. The only motivation was to help other human beings in desperate need. To give and not to seek anything in return except the well-being of the other: that is love, and '*God is love.'* (1 John 4:8).

So, where there is love, there is God.

1. Encyclical 'Humanae Vitae' n.14
2. id. n.17
3. Vatican Council Constitution on The Church, n.12
4. Instruction on Respect for Life in its Origin and on the Dignity of Procreation
5. Instruction concrening the criteria for Discerning of Vocations with regard to person with Homosexual Tendencies in view of admission to the Seminary and to Holy Order.
6. see Chapter 5 on 'The Church'.
7. Karen Armstrong in 'The Case for God' (The Bodley Head, London) identifies the source of this story:Elie Weisel, 'Night', trans. Stella Rodway (Harmondsworth, 1981)

UKBookland gives you the opportunity to purchase all of the books published by UKUnpublished.

Do you want to find out a bit more about your favourite UKUnpublished Author?

Find other books they have written?

PLUS – UKBookland offers all the books at Excellent Discounts to the Recommended Retail Price!

You can find UKBookland at www.ukbookland.co.uk

Find out more about **Rev. Bernard O'Connor OSA** and his books.

Are you an Author?

Do you want to see your book in print?

Please look at the UKUnpublished website:
www.ukunpublished.co.uk

Let the World Share Your Imagination

Lightning Source UK Ltd.
Milton Keynes UK
25 February 2010

150576UK00001B/5/P